Stuart Yarnold

Building a PC

Third Edition

In easy steps is an imprint of In Easy Steps Limited
Southfield Road · Southam
Warwickshire CV47 0FB · United Kingdom
www.ineasysteps.com

Third Edition

Notice of Liability
Every effort has been made to ensure that this book contains accurate
and current information. However, In Easy Steps Limited and the
author shall not be liable for any loss or damage suffered by readers
as a result of any information contained herein.

Trademarks
Microsoft® and Windows® are registered trademarks of Microsoft
Corporation. All other trademarks are acknowledged as belonging to
their respective companies.

In Easy Steps Limited supports The Forest Stewardship Council (FSC),
the leading international forest certification organisation. All our titles
that are printed on Greenpeace approved FSC certified paper carry the
FSC logo.

MIX
Paper from
responsible sources
FSC® C020837

Printed and bound in the United Kingdom

ISBN 978-1-84078-428-2

Contents

1 Before You Start

This chapter will give you useful information to help buy the components you need and from the right sources, in order to build yourself the perfect PC.

Introduction

The picture below will give you an idea of what's involved in the physical aspect of building a computer:

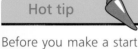

These are all the components required to build a computer system. As you can see there are quite a few of them and, while putting them all together may seem a somewhat daunting prospect, this stage is actually relatively straightforward.

Building a computer also involves two other stages – buying the parts and then having assembled them, setting up your system.

Regarding the former, there are many factors to consider and any mistakes at this stage can result in a computer system that, at best, is not what you really wanted it to be and, at worst, simply won't work.

For example, the memory modules must be compatible with the motherboard and given the proliferation of motherboards, memory types and form factors, it is very easy to get this wrong.

To ensure you make the right decisions and do not end up with problems down the line, this book offers detailed buying guidelines regarding all the major parts in your system.

We then show you how to install them. While this is not difficult, there are certain things you need to watch out for. A good example is the installation of the memory modules. You need to be very careful when doing this as it is very easy to damage them by incorrect handling.

The use of pictures helps to illustrate the assembly stage as clearly as possible. By the time you have finished, you should be looking at something like this:

Hot tip

Computers are modular in construction. This helps to make the assembly stage relatively straightforward.

Finally, you need to set the system up. This will involve altering settings in the BIOS, partitioning and formatting the hard drive and installing the operating system and device drivers.

Many, if not most, problems are encountered at this stage, so we provide full instructions on how to access and set up the BIOS, and get the hard drive and operating system operational.

Finally, you will find a chapter on troubleshooting common problems; this may be useful should you find your new system does not work as expected.

Hot tip

Setting up the system and getting everything to work will, for most people, be the most difficult part of the job.

Store-Bought versus Self-Build

Before you decide to take the DIY route and start spending your hard-earned cash on all the various parts, give some thought to the pros and cons. Building a PC yourself can turn out to be an expensive mistake if things go wrong. Also, remember there are good reasons for buying from a store. These include:

Time
Self-build is going to take a lot longer than simply walking into your nearest store, buying a system off the shelf and then taking it home. To make it cost-effective you will have to spend time finding the cheapest suppliers of all the various parts, which will probably mean dealing with several different ones.

Effort
You have to actually build the PC, set it up and install the operating system.

Aggravation
If the completed system does not work then you have to troubleshoot it. This will take more time and, if it turns out you have damaged a component during assembly, it will need replacing at extra cost to you.

In addition, if you are unable to get the system working, you may end up taking it to a repair shop. All of this is going to involve more time and money. Buying from a store spares you all this potential aggravation.

System Warranty
A pre-built system comes with a warranty, a self-built system does not. If things go wrong, you're on your own. Buying from a store will give you peace of mind.

The advantages of self-build are:

Cost
If you buy OEM parts (see page 13), and from the right source, your PC should be cheaper than buying the ready-built equivalent. However, it must be said that the difference will probably not be as much as you might think and, if saving money is your primary motive, you may find it is simply not worth the bother.

Component Warranties

If you take the self-build route, you will at least have the warranties supplied with all the individual components. These are usually worth more than the PC manufacturers' warranties. Also service from component manufacturers is usually much swifter and more reliable.

Quality

It is a fact that most ready-built systems, particularly at the lower-end of the market, include parts of low quality. Typical examples are monitors and power supply units. Self-build allows you to choose good quality components that will give you a more reliable and longer lasting computer.

Features

Buy a PC from a store and you will, in all likelihood, be buying things you do not need or want. For example, it may come with a high specification video card, which will add considerably to its cost. If you don't play resource-intensive 3D games (which is the only application that requires such a card), you will have wasted some of your money.

By building it yourself, you end up with a system that is tailored exactly to your requirements with no superfluous features or capabilities that will never be used.

Software

Most ready-built systems come with an operating system pre-installed. In addition, there will often be other software bundled with the system. However, this bundled software is often of dubious quality and usually also well past its sell-by date. Much of it is useless to the buyer and so is money wasted.

Most manufacturers these days do not supply an operating system installation disk but rather a "recovery disk", which recreates the original setup from an image stored on the hard drive.

If the image file is accidently deleted or becomes corrupt, the user will have no way to recover from operating system failure.

While, with the self-build route, you may have the additional expense of buying the operating system, it will at least be an original copy that can be used as many times as necessary.

Hot tip

Building your own computer allows you to "future-proof" it to a certain degree. For example, you can choose a motherboard that can take a more powerful CPU than the one you are intending to install. A year or so down the line, when the faster CPUs have dropped in price, you can then upgrade it.

11

Don't forget

Before you buy the parts, think about possible future uses for the PC.
  This may save you money in the long-term by not having to make an early upgrade.

Hot tip

With regard to Windows Vista and Windows 7, be aware that in order to run the Aero (transparent windows) feature, a video system capable of supporting DirectX 9, Pixel Shader 2.0, and 128 MB of memory will be required.

What Do You Want it to Do?

Having made the decision to build the PC yourself, you now need to make a list of all the parts required. This stage of building a computer is probably the most important, as any mistakes here will result in a PC that is not ideal (the whole point of the exercise) or that has to be subsequently modified at extra cost.

However, before you can do this you must establish exactly what you are going to use the PC for, i.e. the applications you intend to run. You then need to buy hardware (CPU, memory, etc) that will be able to run these applications. The table below shows the approximate hardware requirements for some common applications.

Application	Example	CPU	Memory	Disk Space
Operating Systems	Windows 7 Windows Vista	1 GHz 1 GHz	1 GB 1 GB	16 GB 15 GB
Office Suite	Microsoft Office 2010	500 MHz	256 MB	3 GB
Desktop Publishing	Adobe InDesign CS5	500 MHz	2 GB	1.6 GB
Graphics Editor	PaintShop Photo Pro X3	1.5 GHz	1 GB	3 GB
Games	Quake 4	2.0 GHz	1 GB	3.0 GB
Media Player	RealNetworks Real Player Plus	1.4 GHz	1 GB	200 MB
DVD Playback	Cyberlink Power DVD 10	2.4 GHz	512 MB	100 MB
CD/DVD Mastering	Roxio Creator 11	1.6 GHz	1 GB	3 GB

With regard to CPUs, even the slowest model currently on the market will be capable of handling virtually any single application. However, you must remember that in practice you will be running two or more applications simultaneously.

For example, if you intend to play Quake 4 on a Windows 7 PC, you will need a CPU rated at a minimum of 3 GHz and at least 2 GB of memory. We say "minimum" because there will also be other applications running in the background that you are not aware of; these will be using the CPU and memory as well.

OEM versus Retail

Having drawn up your list of required components, it is time to open your wallet. One of your first decisions is whether to buy retail or OEM products.

OEM stands for "Original Equipment Manufacturer" and is a term used to describe a company that manufactures hardware to be marketed under another company's brand name. Typically, OEM products are sold unboxed and with no documentation or bundled software. Also, warranties offered are usually limited. All this enables these products to be sold at a lower price.

The retail versions, on the other hand, will be packaged and supplied with user manuals, registration cards and full warranties. Very often, the buyer will also get bundled software. Most importantly, retail products are far more likely to be the genuine article – remember, there are many counterfeit products on the market.

Retail products will also include things that OEM versions don't. For example, a retail CPU will include a heat sink and fan; the OEM version will not. Retail hard drives will include the interface cable; OEM drives won't.

Another important factor is that of quality. All production lines, whatever the product, produce a number of sub-standard items that nevertheless work. This is particularly so with silicon chips, which are to be found in virtually all PC components. In literally every production run, some chips will be superior to others; these are the ones that will be packaged and sold at retail prices. Inferior chips go the OEM route.

Therefore, if you are looking to build a high quality system, you will definitely need to buy retail boxed components.

If budget is your primary concern, then buy OEM. You will save money, but it could be at the expense of quality. As with all things in life, you get what you pay for.

Something else to be wary of when buying OEM, is that many retailers, computer stores in particular, will try to sell you an OEM component at the full retail price. No one who is computer savvy will fall for this, but many people are caught out and end up paying the full price for an incomplete and sometimes inferior product.

Beware

If you buy OEM parts, be aware that in many cases, you will be buying extremely limited warranties. There is also a risk of getting fake or sub-standard components. Only take this route if you need to save money.

Don't forget

If you want parts guaranteed to be of good quality, spend the extra needed to get retail boxed products. It could save you money in the long run, not to mention unwanted aggravation.

Beware

If you do decide to buy any OEM products, make sure that you are not being conned into paying the full retail price. Be especially wary when buying OEM parts from a store.

Where to Buy Your Parts

Computer Stores

Buying from a store is probably your quickest and safest option. If a part is defective, you can simply take it back and exchange it for a new one. However, it does mean getting off your backside, and does not offer the convenience afforded by the mail order and Internet methods of shopping.

It is a known fact that sales staff in many of these stores, particularly the large chain-stores, can be somewhat limited in their knowledge of computers. Any advice or opinions offered by these people should be taken with a pinch of salt and checked out before you part with your cash.

There is also the risk of being conned into paying the full price for outdated items. While, to be fair, this can also happen with mail order and Internet companies, in practice, it is less likely as these companies exist by undercutting the big computer stores and will take every opportunity to do so.

You will pay the highest price for your components in computer stores, as they have high overheads to cover.

Mail Order

Mail order is very convenient and allows the buyer to compare prices without having to trudge from store to store. In addition, you do not have to keep fending off pushy sales staff.

You will usually find that a mail order catalog has a much wider range of products than you would find in any computer store.

Sales staff tend to be more knowledgeable about the products they are selling and will usually give you better advice than you would get in a store.

Prices will be lower than store prices and this is mail order's main advantage.

Disadvantages include time and distance. The company's headquarters could be several hundred miles away, so if there is a problem you cannot just nip down and get it sorted out immediately. Delivery is done by courier and it is quite common for delivered goods to arrive in a damaged condition. This means delays while the item is reshipped.

Another drawback is lack of information. Whereas in a computer store you can get a lot of facts from the box and associated promotional literature, not to mention actually seeing the product, the details in many catalogs can be on the sketchy side.

The Internet

The Internet has become a real boon to those who build and upgrade PCs. Not only can you buy your parts at the lowest price online, but you can also get a tremendous amount of information to help you make informed buying decisions.

There are sites devoted to all the major parts of a computer system. These offer information such as technical details, troubleshooting, installation and buying guides, etc.
If you are looking for detailed specifications on a particular product, visit the manufacturer's website; all the major manufacturers are online.

Also online are the major computer and computer parts retailers. Their online prices are lower than in their retail outlets.

Price comparison sites, such as www.pricewatch.com in the USA and www.kelkoo.co.uk in Europe, are very useful.

Don't forget

Mail order catalogs and the Internet give you access to a much wider range of products than you are likely to find in any retail outlet. In addition, you will have no sales staff to keep at arms length, so you can browse at your leisure.

15

Simply key in the relevant details and you will be presented with a list of sites selling the product, together with the price. This can save a lot of time when looking for the best deal.

Another advantage is that online catalogs are usually much more detailed in terms of specifications and features than mail order catalogs.

In all other respects though, buying on the Internet is the same as buying mail order. It all relies on courier and postal delivery, and is subject to the same limitations and restrictions.

Beware

Many websites offer products at seemingly bargain prices that do not actually exist. This is a common ruse to get you interested in the site. Sites selling bargain holidays and flights are typical offenders in this respect, and some computer-related sites use the same trick.

Parts You Will Need

The following is a list of the hardware components you will need to build a basic computer system:

- Monitor
- System case
- Power supply unit (PSU)
- Motherboard
- Central processing unit (CPU)
- Memory (RAM)
- Hard disk drive (HDD)
- Video card (see top margin note)
- Sound card (see top margin note)
- DVD drive
- Keyboard
- Mouse
- Speakers

Tools You Will Need

Very little is required in the way of tooling. The following is all you are likely to need:

Screwdrivers
One medium size cross-head screwdriver for screwing the motherboard into place and securing the drive units and expansion cards.

Cutter
For cutting cable ties to length. You will need these to bundle up the internal cables in a neat fashion, so they do not interfere with airflow in the case.

You will also need a supply of cable ties. These are available from any computer store.

Electrostatic Wrist Strap
This item is not essential, but is highly recommended. The static electricity in your body is a killer for the PC's circuit boards; this applies particularly to the memory modules.

Alternatively, you can buy a pair of close fitting rubber gloves such as those used by surgeons. This will serve the same purpose.

2 Central Processing Units

This chapter will clear up some misconceptions regarding these devices, show which section of the market you should be looking at and explain associated terminology and technology.

CPU Manufacturers

Along with the motherboard, the processor is one of the most important parts in a PC and, more than any other, influences the speed at which it runs.

There are quite a few CPU manufacturers, the more well known being AMD, Intel, IBM, Compaq, SIS, Nvidia and Via. IBM and Compaq processors are aimed more at the business end of the market, while Via, Nvidia and SIS are better known for their chipsets, which are found on many mainstream motherboards.

Therefore, as far as the home-PC market and the self-builder are concerned, the choice comes down to Intel or AMD. Both companies make models for high-end, mid-range and low-end machines.

Intel CPUs

Top of the Intel range are the Xeon and the Itanium, which are aimed at the server market. These are seriously high-performance processors and are priced accordingly. For the self-builder they do not really come into the equation.

Next up are the Core i7, Core i5 and Core i3 CPUs (in that order) with which Intel currently rule the Desktop PC market. Also available are older Core 2 Duo, Dual-Core Pentium and Celeron CPU's. We'll take a look at these in more detail.

Core i7 CPU

Intel's flagship product for Desktop PCs is the Core i7 range of processors. In the main, these CPUs feature four processors with Hyper-Threading technology, which creates an extra four *virtual* processors. They also come with Intel's Turbo Boost feature, which increases the CPU's speed beyond the base speed when an application requires a boost in processing power. Effectively, it is an automatic overclocking system. At the very top of the i7 range are several CPUs that feature no less than six cores.

Another i7 feature is an integrated memory controller that enables three channels of DDR3 1600 MHz memory, and thus provides a considerable increase in processing efficiency.

i7 CPUs also have a new feature called the QuickPath Interconnect (QPI) system. This is a replacement for the old Front Side Bus (FSB) and provides a more efficient and faster data route between the processor and the motherboard.

Beware

There is a lot of marketing hype regarding the clock speed of CPUs. However, this is only one indicator of a CPU's quality. You should also consider things like the size of the cache memory, Front Side Bus (FSB) speed, the chip's micron size, and technologies such as Hyper-Threading, Turbo Boost, and multi-channel memory support.

As ever though, the best indicator of all is the price.

Core i7 processors are available for motherboards fitted with either the LGA1156 CPU socket or the LGA1366 CPU socket. Both setups offer the same features but systems that utilize the LGA1366 socket are faster.

In summary, i7's are high-performance CPUs and are intended for power users and gamers who require powerful systems.

Core i5 CPU

Next in Intel's Desktop range is the Core i5 CPU. As with all processor ranges, there are several different models of this CPU. Most of the i5s have two cores (instead of four as with the i7 range). Only the i5-750 and the i5-750S are quad-core CPUs.

However, the i5-750 and the i5-750S do not have Hyper-Threading technology whereas the two-core i5's do. This enables the latter to also have two virtual cores, which to a certain degree mitigates the loss of performance due to having only two physical cores.

Also lacking is triple-channel memory support – i5s use traditional dual-channel memory configuration. Yet another drawback is the use of a scaled-down version of the QuickPath Interconnect (QPI) system used in the Core i7s, which is known as the Direct Media Interface (DMI). The Turbo Boost feature is available though.

To summarize, the main differences between the i7 and the i5 are:

- No Core i5 CPU has more than four physical or virtual cores as opposed to the i7s, which all have either eight (in four core models) or twelve (in six-core models). This means that i5s are not as fast under heavily multi-threaded workloads

- No triple-channel memory for the i5 results in an overall loss in system efficiency compared to the i7

- The Core i7 uses the QuickPath Interconnect (QPI) system, while the Core i5 makes do with the less efficient Direct Media Interface (DMI)

- The Core i5 CPUs have a smaller Level 3 cache memory size, typically 4-6 MB as opposed to the 8 MB of the i7s

Hot tip

Virtual cores do not provide the same level of processing power that physical cores do. However, they enable the operating system to schedule more threads or processes simultaneously, thus increasing the efficiency of the CPU.

Core i3 CPU

The i3 is the baby of the Core i range of CPUs and thus comes with the lowest specifications. As with most of the i5s, these processors have two physical cores and Hyper-Threading technology to create two virtual cores.

Multi-channel memory support is restricted to dual-channel and they don't have the Turbo Boost feature. It is the latter that differentiates them from the i5s. Otherwise, they are similar.

The Core i3 is basically a highly specified budget CPU and provides excellent value for money.

Older Intel CPUs

Prior to the introduction of the Core i7, i5 and i3 ranges, the Core 2 Duo range were Intel's premier Desktop CPUs. These excellent processors are still available and are now very competitively priced. However, good as they are, even the Core i3 provides better overall system performance due to the new technologies built in to these CPUs.

Also still available are Pentium, and Celeron, dual-core CPUs which, as with the Core 2 Duo range, provide very good value for money.

AMD CPUs

At the time of writing, AMD CPUs are generally considered to be not as good as Intel's offerings. Desktop processors are available in two main ranges: the Athlon II and the Phenom II. AMD also produce the highly specified Opteron, which is designed for the server market where it competes with Intel's Itanium and Xeon.

Phenom II

The Phenom II X6 is currently AMD's top of the range Desktop CPU and has six cores. It utilizes AMD's Turbo Core technology, which does exactly the same as Intel's Turbo Boost feature – i.e. providing a boost in processing power when it is needed.

It also has Hyper-Transport Technology, which provides improved access times to system I/O for better performance.

Other features include an integrated memory controller, which enables the memory to communicate more quickly with the system.

Note that no AMD CPU currently supports triple-channel memory configuration. If this is something you require, the choice is clear – an Intel CPU. Also, AMD does not provide a technology similar to Intel's Hyper-Threading so, currently, an otherwise like-for-like AMD CPU will always be inferior to an Intel CPU equipped with Hyper-Threading.

The rest of the Phenom range consist mainly of four-core processors of various clock speeds and cache sizes.

Athlon II

Quite simply, the Athlon II CPU is a Phenom II CPU but without any Level 3 cache, and with lower clock speeds. Accordingly, it offers a lower performance level.

These CPUs are available in four-, three-, and two-core models.

Older AMD CPUs

The AMD Sempron CPU has been around a long time now but with a clock speed of 2.8 GHz, is still a capable performer. This CPU is available in both single- and dual-core models and so can be used even in a multi-tasking environment, assuming the applications being run are not too demanding.

Intel or AMD?

You will no doubt have noticed that we have written less about AMD's CPUs than Intel's. This is for the simple reason that there is less to write about. The architecture of Intel's Core i range is more up-to-date than that of AMD's Phenom range and provides new features, e.g. triple-channel memory support, that AMD haven't matched.

Accordingly, Intel CPUs currently offer superior performance. As an illustration of this, benchmark tests reveal that a four-core Core i7 from Intel outperforms AMD's top-of-the-range six-core Phenom II CPU.

However, it's not all roses in the Intel camp. On a cost/performance ratio, AMD CPUs do offer better value and, for this reason, are the preferred option for many people. It also has to be said that while their processors are currently no match for those from Intel, they do provide perfectly adequate performance.

Hot tip

An important factor to remember when buying a CPU is your possible requirements in the future. While you may not need a powerful one now, you may subsequently develop an interest that does require more processing power. For this reason, it makes sense to buy one with "a bit in hand".

What CPU To Buy?

All computers can be placed in one of four categories: low-end, mid-range, high-end, and gaming machines. The CPU you buy will, to a large degree, be dictated by which of these categories your PC is intended to be in.

High-End Systems
These systems are predominantly servers and workstations, which require the most powerful (and most expensive) processors, i.e. Intel's Xeon and Itanium, and AMD's Opteron.

Home users requiring out-of-the-ordinary performance at a more affordable price, will be suitably served by a six- or four-core CPU such as those from Intel's Core i7 range. The only CPUs from AMD that belong in this category are the 6-core Phenom IIs.

Mid-Range Systems
Home computers are mostly in this class of computer and the range of suitable CPUs is vast. These PCs tend to be used for a range of applications, some of which need a reasonably powerful CPU, and others don't. For example, PC games that aren't too CPU-intensive, office applications, email, and the Internet.

All of these will run very nicely with any CPU from Intel's Core i5 range, a top-end model from the Core i3 range, a mid- to top-end model from the Core 2 Duo range, or a top-end dual-core Pentium.

Suitable AMD CPUs include any Phenom II CPU and mid- to top-end Athlon II CPUs.

Low-End Systems
Basic applications such as playing simple games like FreeCell, email, and web browsing require very little from the CPU. Suitable Intel processors include low-end CPUs from the Core 2 Duo range and dual-core Pentiums. Low-end Athlon IIs from AMD will also fit the bill.

Right at the bottom of the CPU market are Intel's Celeron and AMD's Sempron. These are both available in dual-core versions and offer surprisingly good performance. They are also extremely cheap. However, buying either will be investing in yesterday's technology and really doesn't make much sense as a few dollars more will get you a much more capable Athlon II or dual-core Pentium.

Hot tip

Note that the CPUs mentioned on the right are currently the best choice for hardcore gamers.

Specifications

Now that you have a general idea of what type of CPU is required in relation to your intended use of the PC, the next task is to choose a specific model. This means looking at the specifications. The following are the ones that should be considered:

Clock Speed

This is the speed at which a CPU runs and is measured as a frequency, e.g. 3.0 GHz (3000 million cycles per second). As every action (instruction) carried out by the CPU requires one or more cycles, it follows that the higher the clock speed, the more actions it will be able to carry out in any given period, i.e. the faster it will be.

Be aware though, that there is a lot more to a CPU's performance than just clock speed. For example, you can buy a 3.0 GHz version of both the Celeron and the Pentium; the Celeron, however, is considerably slower and one of the reasons is that it has an FSB speed (see below) of 800 MHz, while the Pentium's is 1066 MHz. So although they both have the same processing power, the Pentium transfers data to the system more quickly as it has a faster FSB.

Front Side Bus (FSB)

A CPU's FSB (measured in MHz or GHz) is a communication channel through which data passes from the CPU to the system and vice versa. Because it is the main data channel in a PC, it is sometimes referred to as the system bus.

All CPUs have a clock speed that is considerably faster than their FSB, so the FSB speed is typically a ratio of the CPU's speed. For example, a Pentium CPU that runs at 2.4 GHz with an FSB speed of 400 MHz, will have a CPU/FSB ratio (known as the clock multiplier) of 6:1.

Without going into the reasons, the lower the ratio, the more efficiently the CPU will work. Therefore, faster FSBs lead to faster system performance.

Note that CPUs from AMD do not have an FSB as such; they use a technology known as Hyper-Transport (see page 25). The same applies to Intel's Core i range – these CPUs have had the FSB replaced by new high speed buses, which are similar in function to AMD's Hyper-Transport.

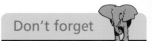

Don't forget

If you intend to buy a CPU that uses the traditional FSB, it is important that the FSB of both the motherboard and the memory match that of the CPU as closely as possible. If the memory's FSB, for example, is much slower than that of either the CPU or the motherboard, a data bottleneck will be the result. This will adversely affect system performance.

Hot tip

If your choice of CPU is one of Intel's Core i range, or an AMD model, you can ignore the issue of CPU FSB speed.

...cont'd

Core i3s and Core i5s use the Direct Media Interface (DMI), while the more expensive Core i7s use a faster version known as the QuickPath Interconnect (QPI) system. As with any AMD CPU, if you buy any of these processors, CPU FSB speed will not be an issue.

However, older CPUs from Intel (Celerons, Pentiums and the Core 2 Duo range) do have an FSB.

Cache Memory

Cache memory is an area of high-speed memory built-in to the CPU, which is used to store frequently accessed data. Since this data doesn't have to be retrieved from the much slower system memory, overall performance is improved considerably. Going back to the Pentium/Celeron comparison on page 23 the Pentium typically, has twice as much cache memory as does the Celeron.

Traditionally, CPUs have commonly used two types of cache – level 1 (L1) and level 2 (L2). L2 is slightly slower than L1 but is larger, and is the one usually specified by vendors. However, modern multi-core CPUs also have a third cache, level 3.

Other factors to consider, include:

Cooling – CPUs generate a lot of heat and so must be adequately cooled by a suitable heatsink/fan assembly to prevent them from burning out. If you buy a retail CPU, this won't be a problem – an approved unit will be included. However, if you buy an OEM CPU, you will have to buy one separately. The important thing here is to make sure that the heatsink/fan assembly you buy is recommended for use with the CPU. If it is not, you could well have heat related problems down the line.

Power – this will be a consideration only if you are buying one of the latest high-end CPUs. These devices draw a lot of power, so you must make sure that the power supply unit (PSU) is up to the job (see page 69).

Technology – Intel and AMD both employ various technologies, such as Hyper-Transport and Hyper-Threading on certain of their processors. These make a considerable difference to both the performance and the price of the CPUs in question. We'll look at these technologies next.

Hot tip

One of the main factors in the price of CPUs is the amount of cache memory they have. This type of memory is extremely expensive and is why two CPUs of otherwise similar specifications can have a big price differential.

Beware

Some of the latest top-end CPUs draw over 130 watts of power. If you buy one of these, you will definitely need to check that the PSU can handle it.

CPU Technologies

Hyper-Transport

Hyper-Transport technology is unique to AMD CPUs, and is basically a high-speed, low-power communication channel (bus) that enables the CPU to communicate with the system at a faster speed and thus with greater data throughput. Effectively, it's a souped-up FSB.

CPUs that employ it have two data channels – one to communicate with memory and one (the Hyper-Transport bus) to communicate with the motherboard chipset. Thus, these CPUs can communicate with both the memory and the chipset simultaneously – CPUs without Hyper-Transport cannot do this as they have only one communication channel.

Another advantage of the Hyper-Transport bus is that it provides a route for the transmission of data and a separate route for its reception. In the traditional architecture used by other processors, a single route is used both for the transmission and for the reception of data.

Note that all modern AMD CPUs are equipped with this technology.

Hyper-Threading

Not to be confused with AMD's Hyper-Transport, Hyper-Threading is an Intel technology that offers improved multi-tasking performance by creating a virtual CPU that appears to the operating system as another, physical, CPU. This facilitates the handling of two simultaneous processes.

Intel claims up to a 30 per cent speed improvement in comparison to an otherwise identical CPU. The performance gain achieved is very application dependent, however, and some programs actually slow down slightly when used with a Hyper-Thread CPU.

Is it worth having? If you do serious multi-tasking, the answer is yes. Otherwise, no.

Note that for Hyper-Threading to function properly, it must be supported not only by the motherboard, but also by the application being run.

In essence, it is a poor man's multi-core CPU – cheaper but not as effective.

Don't forget

If you want a Hyper-Threaded system, you will need more than a Hyper-Thread CPU. For this technology to work, it is necessary to have a Hyper-Thread compatible motherboard, and also software.

...cont'd

Multi-Core

Multi-core Desktop CPUs employ two, four or six processor cores on the same chip. Each core functions and processes data independently and is coordinated by the operating system.

With regard to the actual speed of the CPU, multi-cores do not have the impact one may think. For example, a two-core CPU will not be twice as fast as a single-core CPU; it will in fact be about 50 % faster, and a quad-core will be about 25 % faster than a two-core.

The main advantage offered by multi-core CPUs is much improved multi-tasking and, to a lesser extent, increased performance for multi-thread applications.

A commonly asked question these days is "How many core's do I need?" The simple answer is that for most users a single-core CPU is perfectly adequate. However, given that these are rapidly disappearing from the market, for general PC use a two-core CPU is recommended.

It's only gamers, and power users who run CPU-intensive applications or many applications simultaneously, who will see any benefit from four- or six-core CPUs.

Turbo Boost

Found only on higher-end Intel CPUs, Turbo Boost is a technology that enables dynamically increasing CPU clock speed on demand. Turbo Boost activates when the operating system requests the highest performance state of the processor.

Assuming the processor has not reached its thermal and electrical limits, when the user's workload requires additional performance, the processor clock speed will dynamically increase in increments of 133 MHz until either a thermal or power limit, or the maximum speed for the number of active cores, is reached. Conversely, when any of the limits are exceeded, the processor frequency will automatically decrease in decrements of 133 MHz until the processor is again operating within its limits.

AMD have a similar technology on its high-end Phenom CPUs known as Turbo Core.

Beware

Don't confuse dual-core with dual-processor. A dual-processor system has two separate CPUs, each of which has its own hardware. Thus, it provides much better performance than a dual-core CPU, which has to share associated hardware, such as the memory controller and front side bus.

64-Bit Architecture

All modern CPUs support 64-bit architecture. But what is it and how does it benefit the user?

The term "64-bit" when referring to a CPU means that in one integer register the CPU can store 64 bits of data. Older CPUs, which could only support 32-bit architecture, could store only 32 bits of data in a register, i.e. half the amount. Therefore, 64-bit architecture provides better overall system performance as it can handle twice as much data in one clock cycle.

However, the main advantage provided by 64-bit architecture is the huge amount of memory it can support. CPUs operating on a 32-bit Windows Vista or Windows 7 system can utilize a maximum of 3 GB, whereas on a 64-bit system they can utilize up to 192 GB.

The caveat is that a 64-bit system requires all the software to be 64-bit compatible, i.e. it must be 64-bit software. This includes the operating system and device drivers (this is why more recent versions of Windows [XP, Vista and 7] are supplied in both 32-bit [x86] and 64-bit [x64] versions). Note that most 32-bit software will run on a 64-bit system but the advantages provided by 64-bit architecture won't be available.

So who will benefit from a 64-bit system and who won't? The simple answer is that every PC user will benefit as their system will be more efficient. Don't expect to see major speed gains over a 32-bit system when running day-to-day applications such as web browsers, word processing and 2D games, though; you probably won't notice any.

However, when running CPU-intensive applications that require large amounts of data to be handled, e.g. video editing, 3D games, CAD, etc, 64-bit systems will be considerably faster. Also, if you need more memory than the current limit of 3 GB possible with a 32-bit system, 64-bit architecture allows you to install as much as you want (up to the limitations of the motherboard).

So to get a 64-bit system, all you have to do is buy a modern CPU and install a 64-bit version of your chosen operating system. Don't forget that all your software and device drivers will also have to be 64-bit versions.

Hot tip

Modern CPUs automatically detect whether an application or operating system is 32-bit or 64-bit and operate accordingly.

Beware

If you opt for a 64-bit system, all your software, including device drivers, will have to be 64-bit compatible. Even though 64-bit systems are now common, there are still programs on the market that do not provide a 64-bit version.

Installing a CPU

The steps in this section show an Intel Core i7 CPU being installed. The procedure is much the same for any other CPU though. Whichever you use, just remember that they are fragile devices and successful installation will require a delicate touch.

Hot tip

While it is not impossible to fit a CPU and heatsink/fan assembly on a motherboard that is in situ, it is much easier to do it before installing the motherboard in the case.

1 Lift the socket locking lever to release the load plate

2 Move the load plate out of the way to access the socket

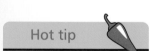

Hot tip

When handling a CPU, make sure you don't touch the connections on the underside. Electrostatic electricity in your body can damage the device.

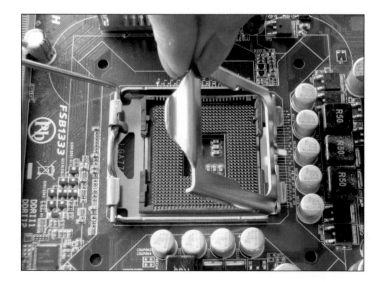

Fit the CPU in the socket by aligning the cut-outs on the CPU with the locating lugs on the socket

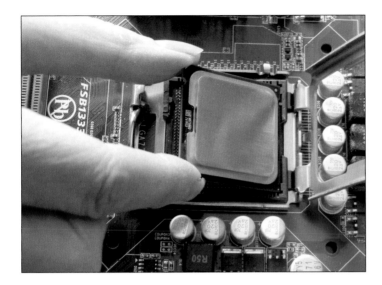

All CPUs are keyed so that it is impossible to fit them incorrectly.

Move the load plate back to its original position and lock it by engaging the locking lever in its catch

Before locking the load plate in position, have a good look at all four sides of the CPU to make sure they are flush with the socket.

Fitting a Heatsink and Fan

There are various methods of securing heatsink/fan assemblies to the motherboard. The most common one employs a simple push-fit into pre-drilled holes in the motherboard. This is demonstrated in the example below.

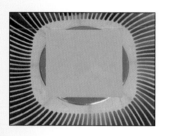

1 Position the heat sink/fan assembly over the CPU and line up the four pins on the assembly with the corresponding holes in the motherboard

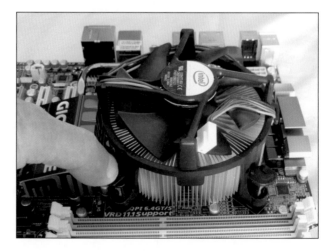

2 Push down on each pin in turn until it clicks into place. Finally, connect the CPU's fan to the motherboard's fan power supply

3 Memory

Memory comes in a range of types, versions and speeds, and picking the right one can be confusing for the uninitiated. Here, you'll learn all you need to know about memory so that you make the correct choice. We'll also show you how to handle and install memory modules.

Overview

As with the CPU, the system memory (RAM) is a component that has a major impact on the performance of a computer system. You can install the fastest processor in the world, but without an adequate amount of memory, all that processing power will do you no good at all.

The memory market can be extremely confusing for the uninitiated as there are many different types, e.g. DDR, DDR2, DDR3, Registered, Unbuffered, ECC, etc.

Then there is the issue of memory form factors. The form factor of any memory module describes its size and pin configuration. Typical examples are SIMMs and DIMMs. Buy the wrong one and it will not physically fit in the motherboard.

When buying memory, you also have to consider the CPU and motherboard that will be used in conjunction with the memory. For the module to function at its best, its speed should be as close as possible to that of both these components.

If you intend to install a large amount of memory, you should be aware that there are limits, which are set by the motherboard and, also, the operating system. If you install more than either can use, you will be wasting some of your money.

However, while all this may sound daunting, choosing the right memory for your PC is actually not too difficult, as we'll see.

Types of Memory

Double Data Rate SDRAM

The memory technology currently in vogue is Double Data Rate Synchronous Dynamic RAM, otherwise known as DDR. The vast majority of Desktop PCs are now using this type of memory as it's cheap, fast and reliable

DDR memory is currently available in three versions: DDR1 (or just DDR), DDR2 and DDR3, and to enable you to determine which is best for your requirements, you need to have some basic knowledge about it.

As with the CPU, memory transfers a given amount of data on every clock cycle. Before DDR came along, PC memory used

Single Data Rate (SDR) technology that only employed the up side of a cycle. DDR, on the other hand, uses the down side as well, thus is able to transfer twice as much data in a clock cycle.

The first version of DDR, DDR1, has now been superseded by DDR2, which is currently the mainstream type of PC memory. The technology behind DDR2 is basically the same as with DDR1; the difference lies in the fact that in DDR2 modules the memory cells are clocked at 1/4 (rather than 1/2 as with DDR1) the rate of the bus. As a result, DDR2 operates at twice the speed of DDR1.

Other advantages of DDR2 over DDR1 include:

- It is more efficient at handling the memory-intensive applications used in today's fast feature-packed systems

- It requires less power (1.8v) as opposed to 2.5v for DDR1

- The lower power requirement results in less heat, and also prolongs laptop battery life

- DDR2 has made possible dual-channel memory configurations, which improve the efficiency with which the memory works

However, the writing is already on the wall for DDR2 as DDR3 is now on the market. The difference here is that DDR3 modules are clocked at 1/8 the rate of the bus, thus they operate at twice the speed of DDR2

As a result, it offers the same advantages over DDR2 as DDR2 does over DDR1. The power requirement has dropped to 1.5v and it enables triple-channel memory configurations to improve even further the efficiency of the memory.

Another difference between the three types of DDR is the form factor. DDR1 has a 184-pin edge connector, DDR2 has a 240-pin edge connector and, while DDR3 also has a 240-pin edge connector, its socket locating key is in a different position.

Because of the difference in form factors, they are incompatible with each other, i.e. a motherboard designed for DDR2 will only be able to accept DDR2 modules.

Beware

Don't forget to check that the memory you buy is physically compatible with the motherboard.

...cont'd

The first table shows the DDR1 modules currently available:

Module	Clock Speed	FSB Speed	Data Transfer Rate
PC-1600	100 MHz	200 MHz	1.6 GB
PC-2100	133 Mhz	266 MHz	2.1 GB
PC-2400	150 Mhz	300 MHz	2.4 GB
PC-2700	166 MHz	333 MHz	2.7 GB

The second table shows the range of DDR2 modules on the market and, from it, you can clearly see that it carries on where DDR1 left off. The slowest DDR2 module, PC2-3200, is faster, and has a higher data transfer rate, than the fastest DDR1 module, PC-2700.

Hot tip

High-performance modules for gamers and power users are also available. These are built to higher specifications and are subjected to greater levels of stress testing.

Module	Clock Speed	FSB Speed	Data Transfer Rate
PC2-3200	200 MHz	400 MHz	3.2 GB
PC2-4200	266 MHz	533 MHz	4.3 GB
PC2-5300	333 MHz	667 MHz	5.4 GB
PC2-6400	400 MHz	800 MHz	6.4 GB
PC2-8500	533 MHz	1066 MHz	8.5 GB

The third table shows what is available in the DDR3 line and, once again, we can see that DDR3 carries on where DDR2 left off.

Module	Clock Speed	FSB Speed	Data Transfer Rate
PC3-8500	533 MHz	1066 MHz	8.5 GB
PC3-10600	667 MHz	1333 MHz	10.6 GB
PC3-12800	800 MHz	1600 MHz	12.8 GB
PC3-14900	933 MHz	1866 MHz	14.9 GB
PC3-17000	1066 MHz	2133 MHz	17.0 GB

On the next page, we look at some variations of DDR memory that are often the cause of confusion to buyers.

Error-Checking Memory

When investigating the memory market, you will also come across other, apparently different types of memory, such as Parity, ECC, etc. We'll take a brief look at these.

- Parity – parity modules have an extra (parity) chip for error detection. This checks that data is correctly read or written by the memory module by adding additional bits and using a special algorithm. However, it will not correct an error

- ECC – ECC modules are very similar to parity modules. However, unlike parity modules, the ECC module will, in most cases, correct any errors it finds, depending on the type of error

- Buffered – buffered modules contain a buffer chip to help the module cope with the large electrical load required for large amounts of memory. The buffer electrically isolates the memory from the controller to minimize the load on the chipset

- Registered – very similar to buffered memory, these modules contain registers that hold the data for one clock cycle before it is moved on to the motherboard

Beware

Error-checking memory modules are not compatible with mainstream motherboards. Boards that are tend to be very expensive.

All of the above modules are based on SDRAM technology and are available in DDR1, DDR2 and DDR3 versions. The difference between them and standard SDRAM memory is the fact that they incorporate some type of error-checking technique that increases their reliability (and hence that of the PC) considerably.

For this reason they are found predominantly in Servers and mission-critical systems. The typical home PC has no need for these types of memory.

Drawbacks are that they are considerably more expensive and are also slower in operation (due to the error-checking procedure).

Don't forget

The types of memory described on this page are not intended for use in a typical home PC. The only users who might have a need for them are those who do mission-critical work on their PC.

35

Buying Memory

When the time comes to make this decision, you should have already decided what type of system you want, i.e. low-, mid-, high-end or gaming, and chosen your motherboard and CPU accordingly. This is important, as to get the best out of your memory it must be compatible with these devices.

You need to consider the following:

Type of Memory

This is the first thing to decide and is a straightforward decision: DDR2 or DDR3 (although we have taken a brief look at it, DDR1 is now, in fact, obsolete).

Just because it is slower than DDR3 doesn't mean that DDR2 is a slouch; far from it, in fact. For the vast majority of users, it provides a performance level that is more than adequate. It is only when considering factors such as "future proofing" and triple-channel memory configurations, and in cases where a high-performance system is required, that DDR3 memory will be necessary.

You should also be aware that high-end DDR2 modules, e.g. PC2-8500, actually provide better performance than low-end DDR3 modules, e.g. PC3-8500 and PC3-10600. This is due to the higher latencies found in DDR3 memory (see page 38 for more on this). However, even with the high latencies, the high-end DDR3 modules, e.g. PC3-14900 and PC3-17000 are faster than DDR2 because of their higher clock cycles, which more than compensate.

Another factor to consider with regard to DDR3 is that motherboards that support this type of memory are considerably more expensive, so affordability may be an issue.

To summarize then, for most purposes, DDR2 is perfectly adequate and, as already mentioned, high-end DDR2 is actually faster than low-end DDR3. However, assuming the higher cost of a DDR3 capable motherboard is not an issue, DDR3 memory is the recommended option, particularly if you are building a high-performance system.

However, whatever version of DDR you go for, the module's specifications need to be in line with the rest of the system. Therefore, you need to consider the following factors:

Don't forget

For typical computer uses, you need look no further than DDR2. Performance enthusiasts will be interested in DDR3.

Don't forget

The real advantage of the huge bandwidths provided by DDR3 memory is only fully utilized in high-performance server systems. Home PCs simply don't need it.

Memory FSB

For the best possible system performance, ideally the memory's FSB speed will be equal to the CPU's, otherwise it becomes a performance bottleneck. The slower it is in relation to the CPU's speed the slower the system will be.

However, modern CPUs have high FSBs, typically 1333 MHz and higher, and the fastest mainstream DDR2 memory, PC2-8500, has an FSB of only 1066 MHz. So what are your options? There are three:

- Buy PC3-10600, and above, DDR3 modules. These do have CPU comparable FSBs. They are, however, expensive (as are motherboards designed to use DDR3)

- Use triple-channel memory. This increases the memory's data transfer rate and results in an effective memory speed increase of about 10-15 per cent

- Settle for a trade-off in terms of cost versus performance

The memory's FSB also needs to be supported by the motherboard. The easiest way to ensure you get this right is to look at the motherboard's specifications, which you will find at the relevant manufacturer's website. An example is shown below:

Boxed Intel® Desktop Board D915GUX	
Form Factor	Micro ATX (9.6" x 9.6")
Processor	• Support for the Intel® Pentium® 4 processor with Hyper-Threading in the LGA775 socket with an 800 MHz system bus • Supports boxed Intel desktop processors with packaging designated by 04B or 04A Platform Compatibility Guide.
Memory	• Four 240-pin DIMM connectors supporting up to four double-sided DIMMs • DDR2 533/400 SDRAM memory • Designed to support up to 4 GB^2 of system memory
Chipset	Intel® 915G Express Chipset

Security	• Infineon* Trusted Platform Module (optional)
	• Wave Systems*
	  • EMBASSY* Trust Suite (optional)
	  • Document Manager
	  • Private Information Manager
	  • SmartSignature*

Audio	Intel® High Definition Audio with flexible 6-channel audio and jack sensing
Video	• Intel® Graphics Media Accelerator 900 • PCI Express* x16 connector (with integrated retention mechanism) provides enhanced bandwidth for next-generation graphics card technology and future headroom
I/O Control	Integrated super I/O LPC bus controller

Peripheral Interfaces	• Up to eight USB 2.0 ports
	  • Four ports routed to the back panel
	  • Four ports routed to two USB headers
	• Four Serial ATA (SATA) channels, via the ICH6, one device per channel
	• One IDE interface with ATA-66/100 supporting up to two devices
	• One diskette drive interface
	• One parallel port
	• One serial port

Expansion Capabilities	• Two PCI connectors • One PCI Express* x1 connector
Network Interface	Intel® PRO 10/100 LAN or Gigabit Ethernet LAN (optional)

The specifications show you the type, speed, and amount of memory supported by the board.

Beware

If you install a memory module rated at a speed higher than the motherboard and/or CPU are designed to handle, the memory will still work but only at the motherboard's or CPU's maximum FSB. You won't be getting the best out of it.

If you install a module rated at a speed lower than that of the motherboard or CPU, this will create a bottleneck in the system as the memory will not be able to keep up. The result will be degraded system performance.

Don't forget

To work in dual- or triple-channel mode, the modules must be identical (many memory manufacturers sell dual- and triple-channel kits for this purpose). Multi-channel must also be supported by both the motherboard and CPU.

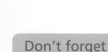
38

Latency

A key performance indicator for memory modules is latency and the term refers to the length of time it takes a module to begin transferring the requested data. This metric is measured in clock cycles and there are many factors involved such as tRAS, tRP, tRCD and command rate. However the most common, and most important, factor is known as CAS (Column Access Strobe).

DDR1 has CAS latencies of 2, 2.5 and 3, DDR2 has CAS latencies between 3 and 7, and DDR3 has CAS latencies between 6 and 10. Fairly obviously, the lower the CAS latency, the better. Remember however, that these figures are relative: DDR2 has higher latencies than DDR1 and DDR3 has higher latencies than DDR2, but compensate by having faster clock cycles.

System builders who want fast memory will definitely need to check this issue before parting with the cash.

Dual- and Triple-Channel Memory

Most current motherboards can run the system's memory in either dual- or triple-channel mode. Motherboards designed for DDR2 will run it in dual-channel mode and motherboards designed for DDR3 will run it in either dual- or triple-channel mode.

Multi-channel mode is basically a method of increasing the memory's bandwidth, which enables the system to run faster and more efficiently. For it to work, the installed modules must all be exactly the same. Note that the memory manufacturers sell dual- and triple-channel kits for precisely this purpose.

However, in most cases, the effective gains made over single-channel memory are usually modest – in the region of 10-15 per cent. It's only in systems that shift serious amounts of data, e.g. servers and work stations, that the full benefits will be seen.

Memory Capacity

The amount of memory that you need in your system is determined by the applications that you intend to run. Don't forget that this also includes the operating system.

The table on the next page provides an approximate guide to the amount of memory required for typical uses of a PC.

Operating System	Low-Usage	Mid-Usage	High-Usage
Windows 7	1 GB	2 GB	4 GB
Windows Vista	512 MB	1 GB	2 GB
Windows XP	256 MB	512 MB	1 GB
Mac OS X	1 GB	1.5 GB	2 GB
Linux	512 MB	768 MB	1.5 GB

Note that 64-bit versions of Windows 7, Windows Vista and Windows XP will need twice the amount of memory specified above. Also, the figures are the minimum amount required.

Low-usage is defined as resource-light applications, such as word-processing, web browsing, email, 2D games, data-entry, etc. If you tend to run several of these applications simultaneously, you should install the amount specified in the mid-usage column.

Mid-usage is running programs such as photo-editing, web applications, multimedia, sound-editing, printing, scanning, etc. If you run several of these at the same time, install the amount specified in the high-usage column.

High-usage is defined as 3D gaming (particularly online gaming), real-time video-editing, computer aided design (CAD), animation, 3D modeling, high-end desktop publishing, etc.

Memory Manufacturers

Unlike the CPU, where the choice is essentially between Intel and AMD, both of whose products are high quality, there is any number of memory manufacturers.

As the memory plays a crucial role in the performance and reliability of a computer system, you must buy the best you can afford – this is not a component on which to economize.

Three manufacturers spring to mind here – Crucial, Corsair, and Kingston Technologies. Buy your memory from any of these companies and you won't go wrong.

Avoid cheap unbranded memory as you would the plague. Poor quality modules cause system crashes and lock-ups, which can be the cause of data loss.

Hot tip

Another consideration is your future memory requirements. Each succeeding version of Windows, and virtually all major software titles, require more memory than preceding versions did. For this reason, it makes sense to add a bit more to your system than you currently need.

Don't forget

For guaranteed quality, buy branded memory from well known manufacturers such as Kingston and Crucial.

Handling Memory Modules

Before you do anything, read the following paragraph:

The electrostatic electricity present in your body is absolutely lethal to memory chips. If you don't ground yourself to discharge it, just one touch can destroy the module.

So, if you have an electrostatic wrist strap now is the time to use it. Alternatively, touch the bare metal of the system case chassis. We also recommend that you avoid standing on a carpet – this is the best way to build up a static charge.

When you do pick up the chip, hold it by the edges as far as possible, as shown below:

Another way to safeguard against electrostatic electricity is to buy a module that comes with a heat-spreader, as shown in the example below. This ensures that you cannot touch the circuitry inside.

Beware

Memory modules are the component most likely to be damaged by incorrect handling. Just one careless touch is all it takes, so be warned.

Don't forget

Memory modules are also available with a heat-spreader. While these are intended primarily as a means of dissipating heat, they also provide the added benefit of protection.

Installing Memory

 The first thing to do is open the retaining clips on each side of the slot/s you are going to use

 Hot tip

While it is not difficult to fit memory modules on a motherboard that is in situ, it is much easier to fit them before the motherboard is installed.

2 Align the cut-out on the module's edge connector with the engaging lug on the slot

 Hot tip

If you are fitting modules in a dual- or triple channel configuration, refer to the motherboard's manual for which sockets to use.

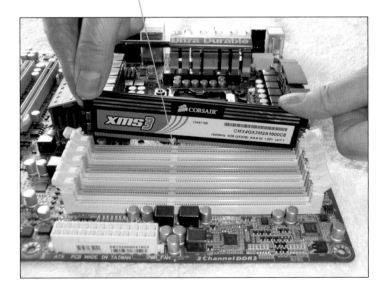

...cont'd

3 Press down on both ends. You will need to exert some firm pressure here

4 When the module is correctly seated, the retaining clips will close automatically

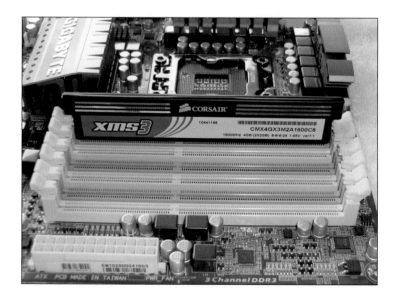

4 Motherboards

This chapter gives you the low-down on the most important board in the PC. Every part of the system is affected by the motherboard, so you can't afford any mistakes here. Read on to discover the available types and what you will need in terms of features and specifications.

BIOS chip

PCI socket

PCI-Express socket

Floppy drive
socket

ATA hard drive
socket

USB connectors

Battery

SATA 2 drive
sockets

SATA 3 drive
sockets

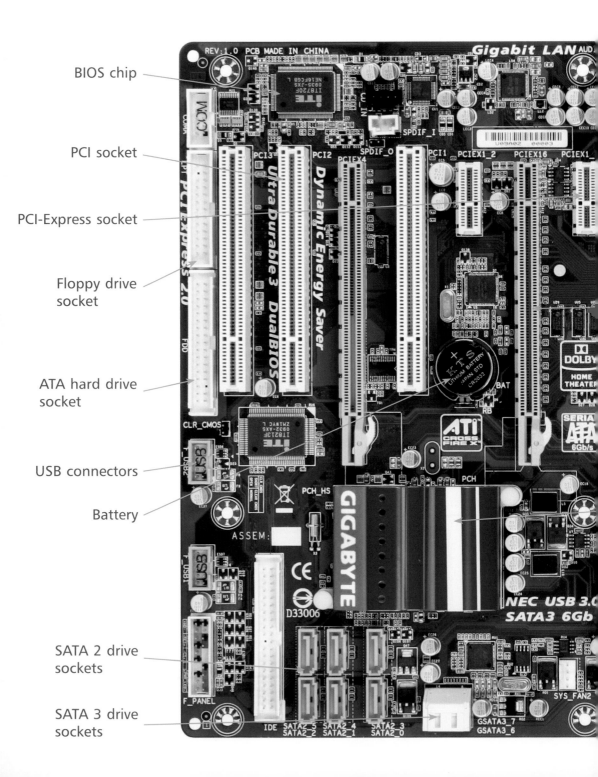

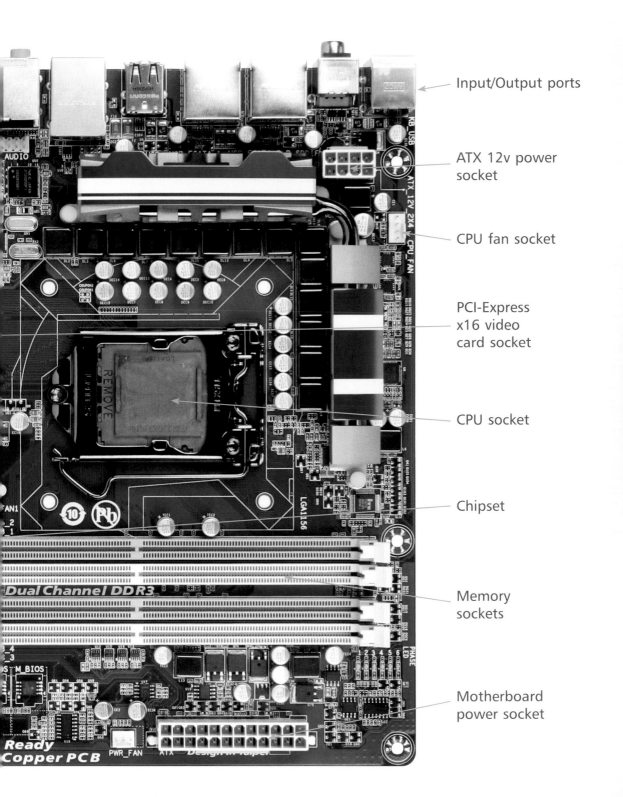

Input/Output ports

ATX 12v power socket

CPU fan socket

PCI-Express x16 video card socket

CPU socket

Chipset

Memory sockets

Motherboard power socket

Overview

Hot tip

The Internet is a mine of useful information regarding motherboards. There are many sites that specialize in benchmark testing of new motherboards as they are released. These tests quickly identify a board's relative strengths and weaknesses. The reviews on these sites are well worth reading.

Hot tip

There are many companies involved in the manufacture of motherboards, and as with most products, whatever their nature, it usually pays in the long run to buy from one that's well established.

Using the human body as an analogy, if the CPU is the brain of a computer, then the motherboard is its central nervous system. Every single part of a computer system is connected, either directly or indirectly, to this piece of circuitry.

Because of this, deciding which board to buy will be an important decision. Not only do you have to consider the features and quality of the board itself, you also have to consider the other parts of the system and how they relate to it in terms of specifications and requirements.

Before we get into what you should be looking for in a motherboard, lets have a brief look at the more important of its functions.

- CPU and memory – the motherboard provides sockets which enable these devices to be connected to the system

- BUSs – these are basically "roads" and provide routes for the relaying of data, e.g. USB, PCI-Express, SATA

- Chipset – this device is the interface between the system and the CPU. It organizes and controls everything in the computer, and is the heart of the motherboard

- Drive sockets – these enable hard drives and optical drives to be connected to the system

- Expansion slots – these enable a system to be expanded by the addition of extra devices, such as video cards and sound cards

- Integration – many boards come with integrated sound and video systems. Other functions that may be supplied include network adapters, RAID hard drive controllers, and utilities of various types

- BIOS – this chip controls a computer's boot-up routines and provides settings for many of the system's components

- Ports – these are found at the back of the board, and provide a means of connecting peripheral devices such as printers, keyboards and mice, USB flash drives, etc

Buying a Motherboard

Before you can make a decision on which motherboard to buy, you must already have made some decisions regarding the components you intend to install in it, i.e. the CPU and memory, and the interfaces that your devices are going to use, e.g. ATA, SATA, PCI-Express, etc.

There are quite a few other factors to be considered as well. We'll start with the CPU.

Central Processing Unit (CPU)

The first consideration regarding the CPU is physical compatibility with the motherboard. This means that the board must provide the socket that the CPU is designed to use.

A quick look at the specifications will ensure you get this right. The CPU's specifications will specify the socket required – AM3, LGA775, LGA1156, etc. The motherboard's specifications will specify the socket provided. They will also tell you which CPUs the board is designed for – you really can't go wrong.

The next consideration is the motherboard's FSB. Ideally, it will be the same as, or close to, the CPU's FSB. However, it's not critical if it isn't. The system will still work but at the lower of the two speeds. Again, you need to look at the specifications.

Don't forget

AMD and Intel CPUs use completely different types of socket. They are not interchangeable – an Intel CPU will not fit into a motherboard designed for an AMD CPU and vice versa.

Beware

Windows 7 and Windows Vista both incorporate technologies and features that must be supported by the motherboard in order for them to work. While older motherboards may well be available at knockdown prices to enable the retailer to shift old stock, and thus be tempting for budget conscious buyers, they may end up with a PC that does not get the best out of these operating systems.

47

...cont'd

Check that the board provides full support for the features and requirements of the CPU. Just because it has the right socket is no guarantee of this. For example, if you go for an Intel CPU that incorporates Hyper-Threading technology, you must get a board that supports Hyper-Threading.

Finally, check that the board can support the clock speed of the CPU – don't confuse this with FSB speed.

A good method of ensuring you get the correct motherboard for your CPU is to go to the CPU manufacturer's website. For example, at AMD's site (www.amd.com) you will find a system-building guide, as shown below:

	Chipset	Motherboard	Revision	Form Factor	Socket
View Detail	AMD 785G	ECS A785GM-M	1.0	uATX	AM3
View Detail	AMD 880G	Gigabyte GA-880GA-UD3H	2.0	ATX	AM3
View Detail	AMD 880G	Gigabyte GA-880GMA-UD2H	2.0	ATX	AM3
View Detail	AMD 890FX	Asus Crosshair IV Forumula	1.01G	ATX	AM3
View Detail	AMD 890FX	MSI 890FXA-GD70	1.1	ATX	AM3
View Detail	AMD 880G	ECS A885GM-A2	1.0	ATX	AM3
View Detail	AMD 890GX	MSI 890GXM-G65	1.0	uATX	AM3
View Detail	AMD 890GX	ECS IC890GXM-A	1.0	ATX	AM3
View Detail	AMD 890GX	ECS A890GXM-A	1.0	ATX	AM3
View Detail	AMD 890GX	Gigabyte GA-890GPA-UD3H	1.0	ATX	AM3
View Detail	AMD 890FX	Biostar TA890FXE	5.0	ATX	AM3

Enter the details of your chosen CPU and you will be presented with a list of compatible motherboards.

Memory

There are three things you need to consider with relation to motherboards and memory.

1)   Can the board fully utilize the amount of memory installed?

2)   Does the board support the rated speed of the memory?

3)   Will the memory modules physically fit on the board?

With regard to the amount of memory, even low-end motherboards will be able to support 4 GB, while most will support 16, and a few 24 GB. As few people are going to need any more than 4 GB, in most cases it should not be an issue.

As far as speed is concerned, ideally the memory's FSB will be equal to the motherboard's FSB. It is not critical though, if it isn't.

For example, if you put a stick of high-speed PC2-8500 DDR2 memory, which runs at 1066 MHz into a motherboard that only supports 800 MHz, the system will still work. However, the memory will operate at the lower speed so you will not be getting the best out of it.

Unless you are reusing an old motherboard or memory module, you will have no problems fitting your memory into the board. Most memory modules in current use are DDR2 240-pin DIMMs, and virtually all mainstream motherboards will accept these. If you are using 240-pin DDR3 modules, you will need a motherboard that provides DDR3 sockets.

Hot tip

Current 32-bit systems can use a maximum of 3.5 GB of memory. 64-bit systems can use well over 100 GB. In practice though, because 64-bit motherboards offer six DIMM slots, and the maximum size of a DIMM module is currently 4 GB, the maximum you can install on these boards is 24 GB.

However, as most home-systems need no more than 2 GB of memory, 24 GB is still an enormous amount.

Don't forget

If you intend to build a power-system that uses a large amount of memory, make sure the motherboard you buy is capable of utilizing it all.

In addition, if you are going to use the latest DDR3 memory, this must also be supported by the motherboard and CPU.

Chipset

A chipset is an integrated circuit on the motherboard that controls the flow of data to and from key components of the PC. These include the CPU, memory, the BIOS and devices connected to the system's buses, e.g. PCI, PCI-Express, and SATA drive sockets.

It also provides a motherboard's integrated functions, such as video and sound systems. The amount and type of memory that the board can handle is also determined by the chipset. So to a very large degree, the chipset dictates the quality and features of the motherboard. Essentially, when you look at a motherboard's specifications, you are looking at the chipset's specifications.

The major players in this particular market are Intel, Via and SIS, and to a lesser degree, AMD and Nvidia. Go with any of these manufacturers and you won't be far wrong. However, chipsets from Intel are generally reckoned to be the best and these are the ones we recommend. Note that this will probably mean going for an Intel system as, not surprisingly, Intel chipsets are usually found on motherboards built to take Intel CPUs.

Front Side Bus (FSB) Speed

A motherboard's FSB speed is the speed at which it communicates with the rest of the system and is also known as the External Clock Speed.

When choosing the board, you must ensure that its FSB matches as closely as possible the FSB of certainly the CPU, and ideally, the memory module/s as well. If it doesn't, the performance of these components, and hence the system, will be degraded.

Don't forget

A motherboard's quality and performance is directly proportional to that of the chipset. Among other functions carried out by this device are the board's integrated video and sound systems.

Sockets

The motherboard's sockets allow you to expand and update your system as and when required.

PCI

For many years PCI was the standard interface for internal hardware devices. However, it has now been largely superseded by the PCI-Express interface. That said, there are still many expansion cards on the market that use PCI, e.g. sound cards and, for this reason, virtually all current motherboards provide one or two PCI sockets.

PCI-Express

This is an enhanced version of the PCI interface that provides much better performance and it will eventually replace the PCI interface. All motherboards provide several of these sockets so if you intend to fit any PCI-Express expansion cards all you need to do is ensure your chosen motherboard provides enough of them. There are several versions of PCI-Express, the latest being version 3.0.

AGP

Used for video cards, the AGP interface, as with the PCI interface, has now been superceded by the PCI-Express x16 interface. It will be found only on old motherboards and, for the system builder constructing a modern system, it is irelevant.

PCI-Express x16

This interface is currently the standard interface for video cards and provides much improved performance over the old AGP interface. It currently comes in two versions: PCI-Express x16, and the newer, and faster, PCI-Express 2.1 x16.

Drive

The current standard interface for connecting drive units to the system is SATA, which has superseded the ATA interface and provides many improvements. All current motherboards provide several SATA sockets. As with PCI-Express, there are several versions, each providing improvements over the previous ones. The latest is SATA 3.0.

Most current motherboards also still provide the older ATA drive interface for backward compatibility.

Even if you currently have no PCI-Express devices or a SATA 3 drive, by buying a motherboard equipped with these technologies, your system will be future-proofed.

If you buy a PCI-Express device, make sure it supports the latest version of the interface – currently version 3.0.

There is also a version of the SATA interface designed specifically for external devices, such as external hard drives. This is known as eSATA and it provides data transfer speeds similar to the SATA interface.

51

Beware

If you decide to go with Mini- or Micro-ATX, remember that the smaller motherboards designed for these systems will provide limited options for the installation of other devices.

Hot tip

Integrated systems have improved tremendously over the last few years and many now offer features that used to be the preserve of dedicated cards.

Form Factors

As with other components, the size, and installation parameters of a motherboard are specified by its form factor. The one currently in vogue is the ATX standard.

Variations of ATX include Mini-ATX and Micro-ATX. These are scaled down versions that are used in smaller system cases. While Mini- and Micro-ATX boards are perfectly functional, they do provide fewer expansion sockets, which may limit your options regarding add-on devices.

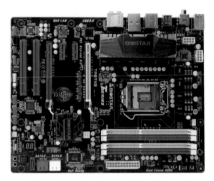

The largest type of case, tower cases, are designed for full sized ATX motherboards, although smaller ones can also be used. Mini- and Micro-ATX boards (shown above) are designed for Midi and Desktop cases.

Integrated Hardware

All motherboards come with built-in hardware, such as sound and video systems. Until fairly recently, however, neither of these has offered much in the way of quality and features. For example, early integrated video did not have 3D capability, which is essential for playing 3D games, and the sound systems could only handle the two little speakers that manufacturers typically supplied.

Today, the situation is much different. The sound systems now supplied with motherboards can support multiple-speaker setups, and the video systems have full 3D capabilities.

For most users, these systems are perfectly adequate for the more mundane and undemanding computer tasks, such as word-processing, email and even 3D games as long as you don't expect top-notch performance.

Note that while nearly all motherboards provide integrated sound, many do not provide integrated video. So if this is something that you require, be sure to check that the board provides it.

Quite apart from sound and video, current motherboards also offer a range of other devices and functions, such as modems and RAID controllers. These represent a considerable cost saving over buying stand-alone devices. Another advantage is that your expansion options are increased as you will have spare expansion card sockets that would otherwise be occupied.

Ports

A computer's ports are the assortment of sockets situated along one side of the motherboard. These allow you to connect peripheral devices, such as printers, scanners and modems.

Most of the ports are standard and are provided with the majority of motherboards. A typical example is shown below:

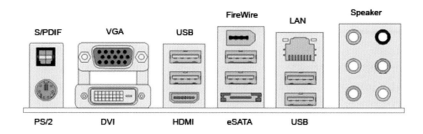

The S/PDIF port is used to connect the PC to audio equipment.

The VGA and DVI ports connect the PC to the monitor.

The PS/2 port connects older types of mouse.

The HDMI port connects the PC to video equipment.

The FireWire port is used to connect FireWire devices such as camcorders.

The speaker ports connect the system's speakers.

The eSATA port connects eSATA external hard drives.

The LAN port is used to connect modems.

Pay particular attention to the USB ports. While virtually all motherboards supply them (usually four), some boards will give you six, or even eight, and with the current dominance of USB as a means of connecting peripheral devices, the more of these you have the better.

While on the subject of USB, this comes in two standards – USB 2 and the new USB 3. There are several differences between the two; the main one being data transfer speed. USB 2 has a maximum transfer rate of 480 MB/s, while USB 3 has a maximum transfer rate of 4.8 GB/s (ten times as fast).

Currently, USB 2 is the standard USB interface as USB 3 has only recently been introduced. However, as USB 3 compliant devices are already hitting the shops, we advise anyone building a computer to make sure their new motherboard provides USB 3.

You will still be able to use existing USB 2 devices as USB 3 is backwardly compatible.

Other Motherboard Features

Multi-Channel Memory

Traditionally, motherboards have provided just one memory channel, which usually results in the system's memory having insufficient bandwidth to keep pace with the CPU, thus creating a data bottleneck.

Dual- and triple-channel motherboards provide extra channels, which effectively double or treble the bandwidth available to the memory. With two or three channels working simultaneously, the bottleneck can be reduced considerably. Rather than wait for memory technology to improve, multi-channel architecture takes the existing technology and enhances the way it is utilized.

Dual-Video Card Setups

For the ultimate in graphics performance, the two main graphics card manufacturers, AMD/ATI and Nvidia, both provide a dual-video card setup. Nvidia's is called SLI (Scalable Link Interface) and AMD/ATI's is known as CrossFire. These employ matched pairs of video cards that operate in tandem to produce vastly improved 3D graphics performance. Their main use, not surprisingly, is hardcore gaming. The frame rate in certain games can be doubled, while the games can be run at higher, more detailed resolutions, without loss of performance.

These setups require a motherboard equipped with two video card sockets.

The BIOS

The BIOS is a small chip on the motherboard that controls the PC's startup routines and provides many essential system settings. It can also offer many non-essential, but nevertheless very useful features. These include:

- A RAID setup utility with which to configure two or more hard drives for performance gains or data protection

- A quick boot utility that speeds up the PC's boot up time

- An over-clocking utility, which enables users to get more performance from their CPU and memory

- A backup utility that creates an image of the system, which can be used to restore the system to exactly how it was in the event of a major failure

Beware

The problem with a dual-video card setup is the cost. Two video cards are required plus a CrossFire or SLI enabled motherboard Furthermore, as these systems are only as good as the weakest link in the chain, you will also need a top-end CPU, and plenty of high-performance memory.

Hot tip

The more expensive the motherboard, the more features provided by the BIOS. Typical features that won't be seen on cheaper boards include over-clocking and backup utilities.

Installing a Motherboard

Your system case may come with a sliding or removable side panel on which to attach the motherboard. The case we are using here does not; however, the procedure is the same.

The first thing to do is locate the plastic bag inside the case that contains various fixings, and rubber feet for the case to stand on. In this bag, you will find seven or eight stand-offs (shown above) to which the motherboard will be screwed. Put these to one side. At this stage you may as well fit the rubber feet to the bottom of the case; it's easier to do it now when the case is empty.

Next, you need to remove the Input/Output cover from the rear of the case, as shown below.

Hot tip

The advantage of a sliding or removable side panel is that it facilitates quick access to the motherboard.

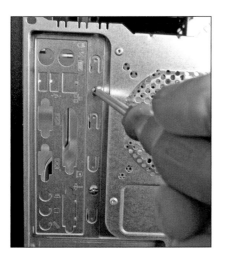

1 Remove the retaining screws

2 Remove the cover

Hot tip

The Input/Output cover is there to prevent you from inadvertently poking things through, which can touch and maybe damage the motherboard. It can also prevent your inquisitive kids from getting an electric shock.

...cont'd

Make sure you screw in a stand-off to support the motherboard at each corner, plus two in the middle. If you don't, when you come to install your expansion cards and connect the drive cables, the board will flex. This can easily break a circuit and trash the board.

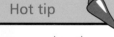

Hot tip

When screwing the motherboard down, make sure that you use the screws supplied for the purpose. If you use screws from some other source and the heads are oversized, you could short-circuit the board.

Now you need to establish exactly where to place the stand-offs. The side panel will have numerous threaded holes, combinations of which will accept motherboards of differing dimensions. Holding the board in place will reveal the ones you want. Screw the stand-offs into these holes. You can do this with your fingers and then tighten them up with a spanner.

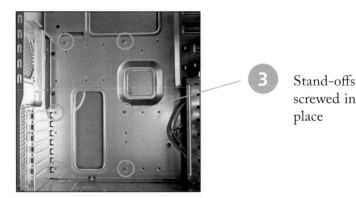

3 Stand-offs screwed in place

4 Using the supplied screws, screw the motherboard on to the stand-offs. Don't overtighten them – this is a PC you're assembling, not a car engine

Finally, refit the Input/Output cover.

5 System Cases

A well designed system case will make a significant contribution to the performance of the PC. We look at what's available in the case market, and consider the features and specifications that will influence your choice of case.

Types of Case

The case is where all the main components of the PC go and is a much underrated part of the system. Apart from protecting the components from the outside world, a well designed case will help to maintain a safe and stable operating temperature; this is crucial for the reliability of a system.

Computer cases come in two main types – Desktop and Tower.

Desktop Cases

These are the smallest and are often used with the monitor sitting on top. This provides their only real advantage – the relatively small amount of desktop space the system occupies.

The downside is that they provide limited potential for expansion (typically, providing only one internal drive bay and two external bays), are awkward to work in and can be difficult to keep adequately cooled.

Tower Cases

Tower cases are by far the most common due to the increased internal space they offer. Not only does this allow more components to be installed, but it is also easier to keep them cool due to better airflow characteristics.

Towers come in three main sizes – Mini, Mid and Full.

Mini-towers are similar in volume to desktop cases, but due to their design, are generally easier to work in.

A full-tower case is the largest size available and provides the most flexibility with room for a large number of drives and other devices.

Mid-towers are a compromise between mini- and full-towers and are the ones found in most home-PC systems.

Note that tower cases are often supplied with an integral power supply unit, which can make them appear to be a bargain.

However, these PSUs tend to be low-quality affairs and our recommendation is to steer clear of them. Instead, buy your case and PSU separately.

Gaming Cases

These are tower cases, but as with all things to do with PC gaming, they are a cut above the average. They provide two important features essential in a gaming system – efficient heat dispersal and looks (aesthetics).

This type of system requires high-end CPUs and video cards, both of which produce serious amounts of heat.

Gaming cases are built to get rid of this by using anodized aluminum (this has better heat transfer characteristics than the steel used in cheaper cases) for the case itself, and an optimized design that maximizes the cooling effect of airflow within the case.

We'll look at the issue of case aesthetics on pages 64-66.

Important Case Features

Capacity

The case needs to have enough space in which to accommodate all your devices, ideally without cramming them in (this can lead to over-heating). If you only need room for one or two hard drives and one DVD drive and have no intentions of ever adding more, a Desktop case will be adequate.

More than this will require a Mini-tower, which can have room for up to five external drives and four internal drives. Very few people are going to need more capacity than this. However, Mini-towers provide little leg room, and so can be awkward to work in.

Therefore, a Mid-tower case is the option recommended as it provides all the capacity you are ever likely to need, is easy to work in, and is not overly obtrusive.

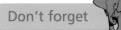

Don't forget

Something to consider if you are thinking small is that Desktop and Mini-cases provide very little in the way of maneuverability when it comes to installing the various parts. This can turn a relatively straightforward exercise into something much more difficult.

...cont'd

Form Factors

System cases are built to form factors that enable them be correctly matched with the motherboard and power supply unit. This ensures that these devices will be physically compatible.

ATX is the current form factor and the vast majority of motherboards, power supply units and system cases are designed to this standard. Unless you want a small system, in which case you will look at Mini-ATX and Micro-ATX cases, an ATX case is almost certainly what will be required.

Cooling

All the system's components are designed to operate within specific heat tolerances, and if they do, you will have no problems.

If your system overheats though, and remember, you won't get any warning messages flash up on your screen, your parts may fail months or even years before they should do. It will also be unstable and prone to crashes, and even loss of data.

Fortunately, for most users, over-heating isn't going to be an issue – the average home-PC, which typically, will have a low-end or mid-range CPU, a hard drive, a DVD drive and maybe one or two other devices in the case, will be cooled quite adequately by the PSU and CPU fans.

However, if you are intent on a more sophisticated system that will include additional or high-performance devices, each of which will increase the temperature within the case, then extra cooling may well be required. Here you have several options:

The simplest is to buy a case that has an integral fan to increase airflow. A gaming case is a another option. For really efficient cooling, you can go for a water-cooled system; these work on the same principle as house central heating systems.

If you decide to go this route, the easiest option is to buy a case with the cooling system pre-installed. Many case manufacturers, such as Koolance and Thermaltake, provide these.

Also available are water-cooling kits, which can be fitted by the user in most system cases. These comprise a radiator, tubing, water blocks (to transfer heat from the components to the coolant) and a pump. Most kits also incorporate at least one fan.

Installation is straightforward with the largest component, the radiator, usually fixed outside to the top of the case. Water blocks are provided for the main heat producing components (CPU, motherboard chipset, and the video card) and are simply fixed to the top of the device.

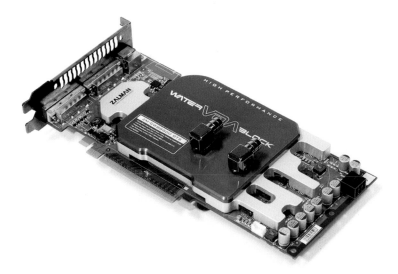

A Zalman water block fitted to a video card

Noise

The downside of cooling is the noise produced by the fans. Single CPU, PSU and case fans are not too bad but a combination of them, and the ones used on video cards, can be very noisy. To overcome this you have several options:

The first is so-called silent fans. Note that we have yet to see one that is truly silent, but they are quieter than standard fans. These are available for CPUs, video cards and system cases.

Also available are temperature regulated fans or a separate fan controller (see margin note). These adjust the fan speed automatically by monitoring the case temperature. The advantage is that the fans will be running at maximum speed (and thus noise levels) only when necessary, i.e. when the PC is heavily loaded.

Note that better quality motherboards provide automatic fan speed regulation.

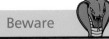

Beware

A drawback with most water cooled systems is increased noise levels as they usually incorporate at least one fan, not to mention an electric pump. However, there are some that are available with no fans such as the Zalman Reserator.

There can also be problems with airlocks, which will need bleeding as with a central heating system. Also, be aware that cheaper systems may not include all the necessary parts – typically the fan/s.

Hot tip

If you do buy a fan controller, make sure it features a temperature monitoring function. This will tell you whether the fans are sufficiently cooling the system. If the computer's internal temperature reaches a critical point, an alarm is triggered in the form of a beep tone, or flashing LED, to signal that the system is overheating.

...cont'd

Beware

The manufacturers of some low-cost sound-proofing kits specify that silent fans must be used. This may make you wonder just how effective the kits are!

Hot tip

If you use one of these heatsinks without a fan, make sure that you check the device's operating temperature. In the case of CPUs (and sometimes video cards), this can be done in the system's BIOS program.

Alternatively, you can get manual controllers, which allow you to manually control the speed, and thus the noise levels, of up to four separate fans.

Good quality power supply units come with automatically regulated fans, the speed of which are controlled by the load placed on the PSU. These provide another option for minimizing noise.

A different method is to soundproof the case. As with cooling systems, you can buy cases that are already soundproofed, or do the soundproofing yourself with a proprietary kit.

Many of the sound-proofed cases currently available are popular

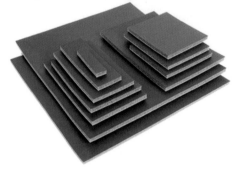

models from selected manufacturers that have been adapted by firms specializing in sound-proofing. They are expensive, though.

The kits are a much cheaper option. They take the form of self-adhesive mats (shown above) that you cut to size and then fix in place. Something to be aware of here, is that these mats can be anything up to twenty millimeters in thickness and can considerably reduce the internal dimensions of the case. Even in a mid-tower, you may well have difficulty in fitting the PC's components afterwards. In a mini or desktop case, maybe not at all.

Yet another option is to replace any fans with specialized heatsinks. These are available from manufacturers such as Zalman, and are weird and wonderful creations of copper and aluminum that provide a much larger surface area to dissipate the heat.

These can be used to replace low-end and mid-range CPU and video card fans completely, or in conjunction with smaller, lower speed, and thus quieter fans.

Note that high-performance CPUs and video cards may still need a fan as well, but lower specification devices will be adequately cooled by one of these heatsinks.

Construction

Cheap models use thin, low-grade steel, which results in a flimsy case with poor heat transfer characteristics. With these you may also find that edges are not deburred, which can lead to cuts and scratches.

Other, typical, problems include poorly threaded and/or misaligned screw holes, which makes device installation difficult, LEDs that burn out after a few hours of use, and low-quality on/off and reset switches, that soon fail or push right into the front panel making it difficult, or impossible, to access them.

Good quality cases are constructed of thicker, higher-grade steel, and high-end models are made of anodized aluminum, which is not only much lighter but also much more efficient at heat dispersement. Many of them also use thumbscrews for quick access to the inside of the case and snap-in fastening methods that make device installation much easier.

A very useful feature for the self-builder found on some cases, is a removable or slide-out tray. These are particularly handy for quickly accessing motherboards that would otherwise require other parts to be removed first.

You might also consider buying a case with a door that covers the front panel. This will considerably reduce the amount of dust that, over time, will infiltrate your CD/DVD drive unit's internal mechanism. Some are lockable, which provides a security option. For an added touch of luxury, you can get cases where the door is motorized.

Some cases also provide a front panel digital readout of the internal case temperature as shown on the right.

Front Panel Ports

Traditionally, a computer's ports have all been located at the rear of the case where they are not easily accessible. Most cases these days supply USB (usually two), microphone, and speaker connections, on the case's front panel. These can be very useful for the temporary connection of digital cameras, MP3 players, etc.

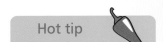

Hot tip

If you do buy a cheap case that includes an integral PSU, our advice is to replace it with a good quality model.
    Some of these PSUs are truly awful and will cause you a lot of problems.

Aesthetics

When PCs first hit the streets, they invariably came in a rather bland beige rectangular box. While perfectly functional, they didn't exactly set the pulse racing. PCs bought from the large manufacturers still tend to follow this trend.

Nowadays, however, there are a huge range of cases in all colors and many different styles. These enable the self-builder to have a computer that is a bit more interesting visually.

If you investigate this end of the market, you will find cases in brushed aluminum, clear and translucent acrylic, with transparent side panels, and some with glowing LEDs that illuminate the case making it glow like a demon's eyes.

Apart from looks, you will also get high-quality construction, usually in anodized aluminum, which as we have already mentioned, is more efficient than steel at heat dispersement.

However, while these cases are stylish and attractive, they are very expensive when compared to standard cases – some of them will cost nearly as much as the parts inside them.

There are available though, many stylish enough cases at a reasonable price, as long as you are prepared to accept a lesser quality of construction.

Beware

Computer style comes at a significant cost. Expect to have to dig deep, if looks, combined with quality, are important to you.

Case Modding

An increasingly common feature found on modern system cases is the transparent side panel, or window.

However, having the guts of the PC on view requires something interesting to see, and this provides a perfect opportunity for customization.

This is known as case modding and it is now extremely popular – people even take their PCs to modding conventions.

So, if you are looking to make a statement with your PC and can't find anything off the shelf that appeals, you will find a multitude of products that enable you to do the job yourself.

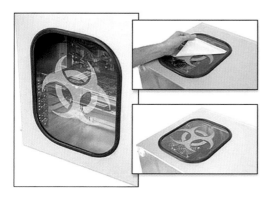

The first place to start is the transparent side panel. Instead of settling for a plain acrylic window, there are a wide range of window decals available with which to jazz it up.

Some, like the example shown above, are simple designs, while others are more complex or ultraviolet reactive, which produce a glowing pattern when illuminated.

Next, you will need to fit a source of ultraviolet light inside the PC.

Hot tip

Many computer parts vendors supply case modding components.
   There are numerous websites that specialize in this field.

Hot tip

If your case doesn't have a side window, you can still do some artwork on the top and sides.
   A quick Internet search will reveal companies that supply vinyl images, which can be applied to the case. Some will take your own images and convert them to a high quality vinyl transfer.

...cont'd

At the risk of taking things to extremes, you can even get UV reactive cable ties.

The standard for PC lighting is cold cathode, a type of ultra-violet fluorescent light that's five times brighter than neon. It is available in many colors, and has the great advantage of not producing heat, a fact that makes it ideal for use with PCs. Just fix the unit in place and then connect it to the PSU (not forgetting to put the sunglasses on first).

Those of you who are really keen can add colored lighting to literally every component in the case. To begin with, all the fans – CPU, video card, and system case – can be replaced by LED or cold cathode versions. Even the fan grilles can be replaced with customized grilles of various designs.

The drive cables can be replaced with ultraviolet reactive cables, while the memory modules can have flashing neon strips fitted at the top.

PSUs are usually dull and uninteresting – buck the trend and go for a model with an attractive case, LED fans, and UV reactive cabling. It won't be cheap but it'll certainly look the business.

If you still can't see clearly, you can add even more lights to the outside of the case. For example, the feet can be replaced with illuminated versions.

By the time you've finished, the computer will be lit up like the Vegas Strip at night. We suspect the novelty may soon wear off but it will be fun doing it.

6 Power Supply Units (PSU)

Power supply units are much underrated components and the wrong purchase can prove to be a very costly mistake. This chapter explains why, and shows you the specifications that need to be considered when buying a PSU.

Beware

A high quality power supply unit will be one of the most important purchases you make. Trying to save a few dollars here could cost you several hundred further down the line.

Hot tip

The power supply unit you buy must be rated in excess of the combined wattage ratings of all the system's components. However, unless you are building a high-powered system with one of the latest processors and video cards, the figures in the guide opposite will be adequate in most cases.

Overview

Power supply units are one of the least interesting components in a computer system, but a good one is absolutely essential for a PC to perform reliably. They are also the part most likely to fail and, when they do, they have a nasty habit of taking other components with them, memory modules in particular.

For these reasons, the PSU is not a component to economize on – if you do, it could cost you dearly in the long run.

Specifications

Specifications you need to consider when buying a PSU are:

Power Rating

PSUs are rated in watts (W) and, as far as typical Desktop PCs are concerned, range from 300 W to about 500 W. What you will need depends on the total amount of power required by the parts in your system. The following is a guide:

- Mini-tower or Desktop – 300 to 350 W
- Mid-tower – 350 to 400 W
- Full-tower – 400 to 500 W

However, bear in mind this is a rough guide and doesn't take into account the power requirements of high-end CPUs and video cards (these two components are the most power hungry devices in a computer system).

A more accurate way of determining what you need is to refer to the following table:

Component	Power Required
High-end video card	250 W
Mid-range video card	150 W
Low-end video card	70 W
High-end CPU	130 W
Mid-range CPU	75 W
Low-end CPU	45 W
Motherboard	35 W
1 GB DDR memory	1 W
ATA hard drive	15 W
SATA hard drive	10 W
SCSI hard drive	40 W
DVD drive	25 W
Floppy drive	5 W
80 mm cooling fan	2 W
Expansion cards	5 W
Fan controller	10 W
USB device	3 W
FireWire device	3 W

Beware

Do not judge the quality of a PSU purely by its wattage rating. This is a common mistake, similar to rating speakers by wattage.

This shows the maximum power (approximately) needed for all the individual parts in a computer system. It will enable you to work out with a good degree of accuracy what PSU your system will need in terms of wattage. Whatever figure you come up with, get a PSU of a higher rating. For example, if you calculate that you will need a 350 W PSU, get one rated at 400 W. There are two reasons for doing this:

First, PSUs work best with a bit in hand. Running one at full load is not recommended if you want it to last any length of time. Second, if you decide later to add an extra device to your system, you will have power available to run it.

Don't forget

It is important to get a PSU that will handle your system's power requirements and still have a bit to spare. This gives you the option to expand the system in the future without also having to buy a more powerful PSU.

...cont'd

Overload Protection

Good quality PSUs incorporate circuitry that will prevent damage to other components in the system, should they fail. These circuits monitor the voltage, current and heat levels of the PSU. If any of these exceed a designated limit, the PSU will automatically shutdown, rather than blowing as cheap models do.

This is an extremely important feature as all PSUs, no matter how good, will eventually fail. If they blow, they will send a surge of current through the system that is quite likely to damage other components – most commonly the motherboard, memory modules, and CPU.

Good PSUs also offer protection against voltage surges in the external AC supply (see page 72).

Cheap PSUs do not offer any protection and so should be avoided. The output voltages of these units also tend to fluctuate, particularly under heavy loads. This can be the cause of general system instability such as crashes and sudden reboots.

So when making your choice, check the specifications and make sure they include protection circuitry.

Form Factor

All power supply units conform to a form factor. You must ensure that the form factor of the PSU you buy matches that of the system case and motherboard. If you are using a mid- or full-tower case, you will need a full-size ATX PSU. If you are using a micro-ATX case, you will need an SFX/micro-ATX PSU.

Cooling

All PSUs have a rear mounted fan that sucks air in from the back of the case to keep it cool. Better models will also have an under or side mounted fan (shown right), which will kick in when the PSU is highly loaded.

This provides extra cooling when it is needed and can also extend the working life of the PSU considerably.

Beware

It is essential to make sure your chosen PSU incorporates protection circuitry that will shut it down when problems occur. Otherwise, it will eventually blow and you may well lose many of the other parts in the system as well.

Connectors

All PSUs supply connectors for the motherboard, CPU, SATA drives and case fans. Most also still provide connectors for older ATA DVD and hard drives. Recent PSUs should also provide a PCI-Express video card connector.

Many high-end PSUs provide detachable power connectors. This enables the user to reduce the messy tangle of unused power cables common in most PCs.

When choosing your PSU, make sure that it has enough connectors, and of the right type, to power all the devices you intend to install. Also, if you intend to fit a PCI-Express video card, ensure that the PSU provides a PCI-Express connector.

Weight

It is a little known fact that the quality of a PSU is directly proportional to its weight. This provides a quick and easy way of evaluating these devices.

A heavy PSU has larger and more capacitors, thicker wires, a larger transformer, larger heat sinks and more connectors than a light one. All of these factors are crucial with regard to the quality of the device.

This specification, typically, won't be shown by PC component vendors. However, it should be available at the manufacturer's website.

Efficiency

The efficiency of a PSU is determined by the ratio of power going into it, compared to the power coming out (the difference is the amount of power lost as heat).

This is an important specification because the less efficient the PSU, the greater the amount of power it will convert to heat. This raises the operating temperature not only of the PSU's components, but also the PC's. The long-term effect will be a reduction in the PSU's, and possibly the PC's, working life.

Efficiency is expressed in percentile, and you should look for a figure no less than 65 per cent. Top-end PSUs will have an efficiency rating nearer 85 per cent.

Don't forget

The weight of a PSU is a very good indicator of it's quality.

Hot tip

A welcome side-effect of a high efficiency rating is less noise. The cooler the PSU, the slower and thus less noisy, its fan/s have to run.

External AC Power Supply

You should also consider the AC supply to your PC. The vast majority of people never give this a thought – it's always there, it always works, so what's there to think about?

Well, actually, quite a lot. AC power supplies suffer from a range of faults, which can, and do, cause problems with PCs. These include:

- Blackouts
- Line noise
- Power surges (spikes)
- Over voltage
- Frequency variation

There are others but these are the ones which most affect a PC. Power surges can cause damage and, in worst case scenarios such as lightening storms, can destroy a PC completely.

Usually though, you won't even be aware of them as, typically, they have a duration of less than 0.001 seconds. They do, however, cause PCs to lock-up and crash. Furthermore, voltage spikes have a cumulative effect and over time will cause components to fail well before they should do.

To eliminate these problems, the following devices are available:

- Surge Suppressors
- Power Conditioners
- Uninterruptible Power Supplies

Surge Suppressors

A surge suppressor (shown right) smooths out any momentary increases in the supply voltage, thus ensuring that the input to the PC's PSU is at a constant level.

Courtesy of Belkin Corporation

As with all your PC's components, it pays to investigate a surge suppressor's specifications before handing over the cash. For example, a good model will also be capable of removing line noise and distortion in the AC signal, thus delivering a "clean" supply.

Surge suppressor protection is rated in Joules; this being the amount of energy that the device is designed to handle. The higher the number, the better the level of protection.

A figure of 500 to 600 Joules will provide adequate protection for home PCs.

Power or Line Conditioners

These devices work by filtering the signal to eliminate electrical interference that can cause noise. They also provide power surge protection and are a step up from surge suppressors.

This is due to the more efficient way they clean up the AC signal. Not surprisingly, however, they cost more and can also be quite bulky in size.

Uninterruptible Power Supply Units (UPS)

These provide the best form of protection and are commonly found in office and corporate environments where data protection is critical.

Apart from surge suppression and power conditioning capabilities, they also have a battery that will maintain power to the computer system in the event of a power cut. This allows ample time to save work in progress and close systems down correctly.

For home users, a good surge suppressor that also has line conditioning capabilities is the device to go for.

Beware

Don't underestimate the adverse effects a dirty or fluctuating AC supply can have on your computer. The way to protect against this is with an appropriate surge protector or line conditioner.

Don't forget

If you do mission-critical work on your PC, or it must be available at all times, you need to invest in an Uninterruptible Power Supply unit.

This device will provide several hours worth of backup power.

Installing a PSU

1 Slide the PSU into position (usually at the top-rear of the case) and secure it with the supplied screws

Don't forget

When you have installed the power supply unit, remember to check that the voltage selector at the back (if there is one) is set correctly. Also, make sure that the PSU's on/off switch (also at the back) is in the "on" position.

2 From the jumble of PSU connectors, disentangle the largest one (this is the power supply for the motherboard) and the 4- or 8-pin CPU power supply connector

Hot tip

Motherboards designed for use with multi-core CPUs use an 8-pin CPU power connection. This provides the extra power required by this type of CPU. Older boards that run single-core CPUs use a 4-pin connection.

3 Locate the power sockets for the motherboard and the CPU (see pages 44-45) and plug in the respective connectors from the PSU

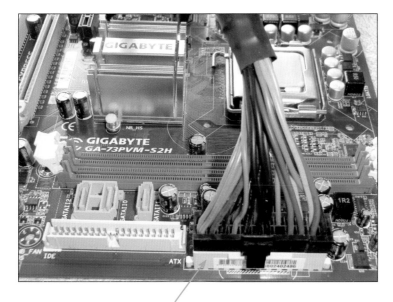

CPU and motherboard power supplies connected

Hot tip

Motherboards designed for use with multi-core CPUs have a 24-pin main power connector as opposed to the 20-pin connector found on older boards. To provide compatibility with both types, modern PSUs provide a 20-pin connector that is paired with an extra 4-pin connector to make up the 24 pins if required.

Note that this also applies to the CPU power connector, i.e. a 4-pin connector will be provided for older boards with another 4-pin connector for use with 8-pin CPU power sockets.

Case Connections

1 Finally, connect the case switches, LEDs and front panel USB sockets to the motherboard. These are in a bank of connectors, usually at the bottom-right of the board

2 Power and reset buttons, USB front panel sockets, power and hard drive LED cables connected to the motherboard

Hot tip

It's very easy to get these connections wrong. While the following is not guaranteed to be the same as on your system, it will give you a guide:

- The PLED connector powers the case power LED and connects to the PLED pins

- The RESET SW connector powers the reset switch and connects to the RESET pins

- The HDD LED connector powers the hard drive LED and connects to the HDLED pins

- The POWER SW connector powers the case on/off switch and connects to the PWRBTN pins

- The SPEAKER connector powers the case speaker and connects to the SPEAKER pins

7 Video Systems

The video card market can be a daunting place for the uninitiated. All the hype surrounding these devices further muddies the waters. This chapter cuts through the hype, explains the difference between integrated video and sound cards, and shows you how to choose a card that will be right for your system.

Video Systems

A computer's video system is responsible for converting the stream of binary 0s and 1s from the CPU into an intelligible picture that is then passed on to the monitor.

Two types of system are used:

- Integrated video
- Video cards

Integrated Video

Integrated video is provided by the motherboard chipset. This is the type of video system commonly supplied by manufacturers of cheaper systems, as it negates the need for a separate video card that would add to the cost of the computer.

However, as video processing needs a processor and plenty of memory, and integrated video doesn't have a processor and little, or even no, memory, it has to use the system's CPU and memory. The effect of this is that the system as a whole takes a performance hit.

Also, as this type of system is primarily about cutting costs, the quality of the video produced has traditionally been on the poor side and usually only capable of producing two-dimensional displays. 3D video, such as games, has usually required the use of a dedicated video card.

However, over the last few years, the quality of integrated video systems has improved dramatically, to the point where they now all offer 3D capabilities. In fact, they are better than many of the video cards of not so many years ago.

That said, they still don't offer anything approaching the power and features of current video cards and, as such, are only good enough for graphics applications that are not too demanding.

For users who only want a basic system for office functions, multimedia and email, etc, integrated video will be quite adequate, and will save you the cost and bother of buying and installing a video card. You can even play 3D games as long as you accept that you will not get the best out of them in terms of frame rate, graphic effects and resolution.

Don't forget

Integrated video is fine for run-of-the-mill applications. For more demanding stuff, however, such as the latest 3D games, a dedicated video card will provide much better performance.

Video Cards

There are two types of video card – the much touted gaming cards familiar to most people, and workstation cards. The vast majority of the ones on the market are the gaming cards.

They both provide a much higher level of video quality than integrated systems do. They have their own processor and memory and so are not reliant on the system's CPU and memory. As a result, the system's overall performance level is better.

Gaming cards are designed with speed as one of the main criteria and provide features that are geared specifically to getting the best out of resource intensive 3D games.

Workstation video cards are intended for heavy duty stuff and provide a greater level of accuracy and performance. For example, they can supply seriously high resolutions, which are needed by some business applications.

They are tested and certified for use with major 3D and video applications. The manufacturers also offer much better technical support. Typical applications are professional level desktop publishing, computer aided drawing (CAD) and real time video editing.

While 3D is catered for, they offer exceptional 2D performance, which is usually far more important in a business environment.

Hot tip

Video cards are much the same as CPUs regarding pricing. Every six months or so, a new batch appears on the market at a premium price that is out of most peoples' price range.

Fortunately, this drives the price of earlier models down to a level that is much more affordable. Unless you want a cutting-edge system, the advice here is to buy a card that is six months to a year old. You will pay much less than you would for one of the latest models, while the difference in performance will be negligible.

Remember, also, what we said at the beginning of the book about hardware technology advancing at a rate with which software cannot keep up. This is particularly true of video cards, and even models a year or more old, have capabilities that many of the latest games and applications are not able to fully utilize.

2D versus 3D

It is all too easy to be taken in by the hype surrounding video cards and lose sight of the basics. While there is no dispute regarding the importance of 3D video, it is a fact that it's only critical to hardcore gamers and a handful of other applications. For most PC uses, and hence users, good 2D video is actually the more important of the two.

So before you succumb to the slick marketing, ask yourself what it is that you spend the majority of your computing time doing. Is it playing 3D games or more mundane stuff such as basic Windows operations, office applications, email and web browsing, etc?

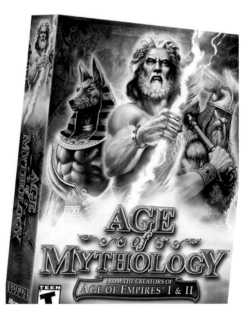

If it's the latter, then you need to be more concerned with your computer's 2D capabilities.

They are the type of things that 3D has little effect on, whereas 2D does. Good 2D performance will improve image quality, text will be sharper and basic things such as window manipulation will be quicker.

While integrated video provides reasonable 2D performance it is nowhere near as good as that provided by a video card. This is why power and corporate users, who often have no need for 3D, will always have a high-quality video card in their system.

Beware

Video cards are the most hyped part of a computer system and, if you listen to it, you'll probably end up buying an expensive model that provides a level of performance that you are never going to need.

80

Don't forget

For the majority of users, good 2D performance is of far more importance than 3D. While an integrated video system will give you reasonably good 2D, a video card will improve 2D performance tremendously.

The Video Card Market

When you investigate the video card market, you'll quickly notice that there are a tremendous number of cards on offer, and may wonder how on earth you're going to pick one out.

However, the choice is not nearly as big as it may appear. This is because many of the cards are, to all intents and purposes, identical. The reason for this is that virtually all of them use the same basic architecture – the global processing unit (GPU), otherwise known as the chip.

For example, take the following cards:

- Asus ATI Radeon 5870,
- Sapphire ATI Radeon 5870
- XFX ATI Radeon 5870

Although they are three different cards from three different manufacturers, they are essentially the same because they are all driven, and controlled by, the Radeon 5870 chip. The only differences between them will be in the quality of the manufacturer's control circuitry and the specifications of associated components. For example, the Asus may offer 2 GB of memory, while the Sapphire may have only 1 GB.

The vast majority of the chips used by video card manufacturers are provided by two companies: ATI (the Radeon) and Nvidia (the GeForce). Note that ATI have recently been taken over by AMD, but many of their products as still advertised as being from ATI.

Both companies offer several versions of each chip they produce – low-end, mid-range and high-end, to cater for different sections of the market. For example, AMD/ATI offers three versions of the Radeon 9800 – the 9800 (low-end), the 9800 PRO (mid-range), and the 9800 XT (high-end).

The differences between the chip versions are determined largely by the following specifications:

- Processor clock speed
- Memory capacity
- Memory type
- Memory clock speed
- The interface used

Hot tip

In most cases, the chip used is specified in the product name, e.g. the Chaintech GeForce FX 5500. Here, the manufacturer is Chaintech, the video chip is the GeForce, and the chip version is FX5500.

Video Card Specifications

We will concentrate here on gaming cards. Workstation cards are really a different entity as they are designed specifically for business applications.

Quadro workstation video card from Nvidia

When shopping for a video card, you need to consider the following specifications:

Processor Clock Speed

This is often referred to as the Core Clock Speed in the specifications and relates to the speed at which the Global Processing Unit (GPU) runs. As with a CPU, the faster it is, the faster the speed and the better the performance of the card.

Low-end video cards have a GPU running at about 550 MHz, mid-range cards at 700 MHz, and the latest top-end cards up to 950 MHz.

Memory Capacity

A video card's memory capacity is sometimes referred to as the Frame Buffer in the specifications. A common misconception is that the more memory a video card has, the faster it will run. However, memory capacity has absolutely no effect in this regard. What it does do is enable high resolutions, and video quality to be set at high levels.

If the application being run does not need a high quantity of memory, an otherwise identical card with 1 GB of memory will perform just as well as one with 2 GB.

Top-end video cards currently have 2 GB of memory, mid-range cards have 1 GB and low-end cards have 512 MB.

Memory Type

Virtually all video cards currently on the market use a type of DDR memory known as GDDR (Graphics Double Data Rate). This is a derivative of the standard DDR memory used for PCs, which has been optimized for use with video. This memory is available in various versions ranging from GDDR1 to GDDR5.

GDDR1 and 2 are now obsolete but there are still many video cards on the market using GDDR3 and 4. Recent high-end cards all use GDDR5.

Given that GDDR5 offers major improvements over GDDR4, this is the memory standard to go for.

Memory Speed

In the same way that high-speed system memory increases the speed and performance of a computer, high-speed video memory does the same for video cards.

Low-end cards come in at around 800 MHz, mid-range cards at 2 GHz and the latest high-end cards at up to 5 GHz.

Interfaces

There are two separate interfaces to be considered with regard to video cards. The first is built-in and provides an internal link between the video card's processor (GPU) and its memory. It refers to how much data, in bits, can be read from, and written to, the memory in one clock cycle.

High-end cards have a memory interface of 512 bits, mid-ranged cards have an interface of 256 bits, and low-end cards have a 128 bit interface.

The second is the card's physical interface. Due to the high amounts of data involved with video, video cards need a dedicated high-bandwith bus, and the one currently in use is the PCI-Express 2.1 x16 bus.

Hot tip

Don't confuse the GDDR memory used by video cards with the DDR memory used by computer systems. They are not the same.

...cont'd

> ### Hot tip
>
> The PCI-Express interface provides sockets of various sizes – x1, x2, x4, and x16. PCI-Express video cards use the x16 socket.

This has a data throughput rate of 500 MBps, and while this figure may not seem particularly impressive it is important to realise that the PCI-Express x16 interface provides 32 data channels (two for each of the 16 lanes). As the data throughput figure mentioned above applies to each channel, PCI-Express 2.1 x16 (the latest version) has a total data throughput of 16 GB per second (500 MBps x 32).

Nothing stands still in the world of computer hardware though, and PCI-Express 3.0 x16, which will have a data throughput rate of 1 GBps per channel, plus some other major improvements, is soon to be released.

This raises the question "Should I wait until version 3.0 is available before building my new system?". For the vast majority of users the answer to this has to be no as there is no current software that fully utilizes the capabilities of version 2.1, never mind version 3.0.

Finally, a note about the old AGP video card interface. While it is now out-dated technology, there are still video cards on the market that use it. Don't make the mistake of buying one of these – PCI-Express 2.1 x16 is what you want.

Other Factors to Consider

Ports

Video cards come with a range of input and output ports, the quantity and type of which depend on the quality of the card and, also, how modern it is.

Older cards will have a VGA port and possibly a VIVO (also known as TV-Out) port.

More recent cards will have a DVI port, probably a VGA port and maybe a VIVO port.

Higher-end cards often come with two DVI ports. Modern high-end video cards will have two DVI ports, a HDMI (High-Definition) port, and the new DisplayPort.

Above, we see a typical video card output panel with a white DVI port, a blue VGA port and a black VIVO port.

Below, we have a modern high-end video card with two DVI ports on the right, a HDMI port in the middle and a DisplayPort on the left.

Digital Video Interface (DVI)
The DVI port is designed for use with LCD monitors, which need a digital signal.

Video-in/Video-out (VIVO)
The VIVO (video in/video out) port enables you to hook up the PC to other video devices such as a television set. More recent video cards now provide a HDMI port for this purpose.

Video Graphics Array (VGA)
The blue VGA port was designed for use with old CRT monitors. However, it can be used with LCD monitors as well.

HDMI
Used to connect video equipment, such as TVs and video recorders, to the PC. It replaces the older VIVO port.

DisPlayPort
DisplayPort is a new display interface designed to replace digital (DVI) and analog (VGA) ports in computer monitors and video cards. Currently only found on the latest cards.

...cont'd

Beware

If you go for one of the latest video cards, make sure it will leave room for the other devices you intend to install. Some of these cards come with quite monstrous cooling systems that will occupy an inordinate amount of space in the case.

Dimensions

Many of the top-end video cards are serious pieces of circuitry and by this we don't just mean specifications, we mean big, as in take up a lot of room. This is further compounded by the also serious cooling systems these cards require.

While you will have no trouble fitting even the largest video card into a full size tower case, with anything smaller you may struggle to accommodate one. So if you are planning on incorporating a high-end video card into your system, make sure that the card will fit.

Note that many gaming cases are designed to eliminate this issue; the Antec Nine Hundred case being a good example. This case allows the drive cages to be relocated to different positions thus creating room for a bulky video card if necessary.

Application Programming Interfaces (APIs)

APIs are basically a set of routines that programmers use to ensure that their software is supported by as wide a range of hardware setups as possible. In relation to video, they allow multimedia applications to utilize hardware acceleration features provided by video systems.

For the API, and thus the application, to work, it must be supported by the PC's video system.

There are various APIs, such as OpenGL and Microsoft's DirectX. The latter is the one most commonly used, so you should ensure that your video card supports the latest version of it (currently version 11).

Power and Heat Issues

Power and heat are only issues if you are buying at the top end of the video card market.

The more features packed into a video card, the more power required to run it. You need to consider this when purchasing the power supply unit. You may, for example, find that you need a 500 watt PSU instead of a 400 watt version – the extra 100 watts to cover the power requirement of the card.

Furthermore, all this power generates lots of heat. While the card's cooling system will keep the card itself cool, this heat will raise the temperature in the system case, and because of this, you may need to install extra fans or invest in a more efficient cooling system.

Noise

There's no getting away from the fact that high-end video cards can be rather intrusive in terms of the noise their cooling fans make.

However, there are ways to reduce, or even eliminate, this. For example, noisy fans can be replaced with silent versions, sound-proofing kits can reduce noise levels considerably; while opting for a water-cooled system or a high-end fanless heatsink, does away with the need for fans completely.

Bundled Extras

Many video cards come with "extras" that can help to soften the impact on your wallet. The most typical example is the inclusion of one or two PC games.

Hot tip

Microsoft release updated versions of DirectX periodically. You can find out what the latest version is (and download it) by going to www.microsoft.com.

Hot tip

Most video cards include a couple of games in the box. While they are never the latest, some of them are fairly recent. If you are torn between two cards, the games on offer might be the deciding factor.

Installing a Video Card

The procedure is the same whether you are installing an AGP card or a PCI-Express x16 card. Here, we are using the latter.

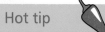 Locate the colored PCI-Express x16 (or AGP) socket

In the case of an AGP card, you will need to open the retaining clip before installing the card, as shown below.

2 Slide the card into the socket. When it is fully inserted the retaining clip will automatically lock it in place

3 Screw the backplate to the case chassis

...cont'd

4 If the card requires a dedicated power supply, connect the 4-pin PCI-Express power connector from the PSU

Having installed the video card, you now need to connect the monitor to it – see page 100. It will also need setting up in the BIOS – see page 157.

When you run the system for the first time, you will have to install the card's driver and configure it to suit your applications.

8 Monitors

There's a lot more to computer monitors

than meets the eye. Read on to get the

low-down on these essential devices and

learn how to choose a good one.

Overview

Considering it gets more attention than any other part of a computer system, it is surprising just how many people pay scant regard to the monitor when purchasing their PC. Usually, the CPU and the video system are of much more interest to them.

This fact is well known to manufacturers and they take advantage by tending to supply rather cheap monitors with their pre-built systems, as they do with keyboards and mice. Typically, these monitors will provide inferior picture quality, low viewing angles and poor power regulation.

However, it must be said that for typical home applications they are perfectly adequate and for the self-builder looking to save money where possible, these low-end monitors do provide an opportunity to do this, as long as he or she is prepared to put up with their limitations.

Those of you who want a better class of monitor, or require one for a specific purpose, will need to investigate the monitor market in some depth as there are literally thousands to choose from.

Types of LCD Panel

With the demise of CRT monitors, all monitors on the market are now of the active matrix LCD type. However, few buyers realize that there are several different types of panel used in LCD monitors. Any buyer looking for a high quality model needs to be aware of this.

Twisted Nematic (TN)

TN panels are cheap to manufacture and have the added bonus of very fast response times (2 to 5 ms).

The main drawback of TN is its color reproduction. As it represents colors using only 6 bits per RGB color, it is unable to display the full 16.7 million colors available in 24-bit true color. TN panels get round this limitation by using a simulating technique called dithering, which is essentially a compromise between quality and cost.

Other issues with TN is that its viewing angles and contrast ratios are the worst of any current LCD panel technology.

Vertical Alignment (VA)

There are several types of VA technology such as S-PVA and MVA, and they all offer better color reproduction than TN panels as they have higher contrast ratios (which results in more accurate black levels). They also offer wider viewing angles.

However, they suffer from two inherent problems: First, their response times are the worst of all the various types of panel and, second, they are afflicted by "color shifting", which is when the image changes, or shifts, when viewed from a slightly different angle, causing uneven brightness levels across the display.

In Plane Switching (IPS)

IPS panels are the best overall LCD technology for image quality, color accuracy and viewing angles (up to 178 degrees). Their only drawback is slightly slower response times than provided by TN panels.

However, this is only likely to be an issue for hardcore gamers who require the fastest possible response times. For all other PC uses and, hence, users, IPS panels are, without doubt, the best choice.

Hot tip

The type of panel used in a monitor is not usually specified in advertising literature. To find this out, you may need to visit the manufacturer's website and look at more detailed specification sheets.

...cont'd

Summary

If your primary interest is gaming, a TN monitor has to be the choice because of the fast response times. The low cost is an added bonus. A TN monitor will also be suitable for typical home PC applications as the image quality, while not the best, is perfectly adequate.

Note that the vast majority of monitors use this type of panel.

Users who require professional quality graphics, need to look at IPS monitors. However, they will have to dig deep into their pockets because these monitors are expensive.

VA monitors offer image quality and viewing angles that are better than TN but not as good as IPS. These monitors will appeal to users who want something better than the mainstream TN offerings but don't want to pay the premium demanded by the high-end IPS monitors.

Monitor Specifications

Having decided on what type of panel technology is suitable for your requirements (TN in all likelihood), you now need to take a look at general monitor specifications. The following are the most important ones:

Resolution

A monitor's resolution is the number of pixels that comprise the image, and is expressed in terms of width x height. Common resolutions are 1280 x 1024, 1600 x 1200 and 1920 x 1200.

All LCD monitors can display several resolutions. However, they can only display one resolution at high quality; this is known as its native resolution. The others are achieved by a process called interpolation (scaling of the image), which reduces image quality.

Due to this limitation, the screen size of the LCD monitor you buy will be determined largely by its native resolution – it must be one that you are comfortable with and that is suitable for your applications.

Don't forget

LCD monitors can only produce a high quality image at one resolution, known as the Native resolution. Make sure that this is suitable for your needs.

The native resolution for the various sizes of LCD monitors are as follows:

- 17- and 19-inch monitors – native resolution 1280 x 1024
- 20- and 21-inch monitors – native resolution 1600 x 1200
- 23-inch monitors – native resolution 1920 x 1200
- 27-inch monitors – native resolution 2560 x 1440

While on the subject of resolution, increasing numbers of monitors are now sold as high definition (HD) models. These monitors have the wide-screen aspect ratio of 16:9 as opposed to the traditional 4:3 ratio.

Resolutions that are classed as HD are 1024 x 768, 1280 x 720, 1366 x 768 and 1920 x 1080

Hot tip

Note that the monitor resolutions shown on the left relate to standard models. Wide-screen monitors have different resolutions.

If you are considering buying a wide-screen HD monitor to watch HD movies or play HD games, you should be aware that in order to watch HD at its best quality, you will need a monitor with a native resolution of 1920 x 1080.

While the other resolutions mentioned above all have the correct aspect ratio for HD, they are not capable of full HD quality because of their lower pixel count.

Don't forget

For the best quality HD video, your monitor must have a native resolution of 1920 x 1080

...cont'd

Response Rate

A monitor's response rate is defined as the length of time it takes for its pixels to go from an active state (black) to an inactive state (white) and back to black again. Basically, it is a measure of how fast the monitor can respond to changes in the data coming from the video system.

If the response rate is too slow, the transition from one picture (or frame) to another can produce an after-image or blurring effect. This problem can occur not only when looking at video, but also when scrolling in an open window.

The generally accepted maximum response rate is 16 ms; any higher and ghosting is likely to be seen. However, it must be said that this is much less of an issue than it used to be as virtually all current monitors have response rates of 5 ms or less. It's only gamers who really need to be concerned about this.

On a related note, LCD monitors with a refresh rate of 120 HZ are now becoming available. These provide much smoother graphics and faster response rates than mainstream monitors, which have the traditional 60 HZ refresh rate. This is something that will be of interest to gamers and those who use their PC for other video related applications.

Contrast Ratio

This is the measurement of the difference in light intensity between the brightest (white) and darkest (black) tones, and it provides a good indication of an LCD's image quality. A high contrast ratio will result in an image that is vibrant and colorful. If it is too low, the image will look faded and washed-out.

Note that manufacturers usually quote two contrast ratios in the specifications The first, typically around 1000:1, is the true figure (the one to take note of) and is always much lower than the second (the dynamic contrast ratio), which can be as high as 1,000,000:1.

To explain this, monitor manufacturers' use the contrast ratio specification as a marketing tool on the basis that higher figures result in higher sales. Basically, the dynamic contrast ratio is a theoretical maximum that the monitor is supposedly capable of. However, it is not a "real world" figure and can be ignored.

Beware

Ignore the dynamic contrast ratio figure; this relates only to the manufacturer's desire to make the monitor appear more highly specified than is actually the case.

What you, as a buyer, are looking for is a true contrast ratio of no less than 1000:1.

Brightness

A monitor's brightness is the measure of the brightest white the monitor can display and is usually quoted in Candelas per square meter (cd/m2). For typical PC uses, 250-300 cd/m2 is quite adequate.

You will only need a higher figure when the monitor is used in brightly lit environments or is exposed to direct sunlight.

Pixel Pitch

This is a measure of the distance between the individual pixels that comprise the display and is another good indicator of a monitor's image quality. The lower the figure, the greater the sharpness and color clarity of the displayed image.

High-quality LCDs have a dot pitch around 0.24 mm, while low-end models will be around 0.3 mm.

Viewing Angle

When an LCD monitor is viewed from an off-center position, there may be a noticeable loss of image quality. The position, in degrees, when this becomes noticeable is known as the viewing angle.

This is not as much of an issue as it used to be as modern monitors have much improved viewing angles. If the user always views the monitor from a central position, and never shares the it with another user (who would have to view it at an angle), it is not an issue at all.

Viewing angles are quoted in horizontal and vertical fields and will usually look like this in specification sheets:

Image Max H-View Angle – 180
Image Max V-View Angle – 170

Currently, the majority of monitors on the market have good viewing angles, similar to the above. However, there are also many with viewing angles as low as 80. So if this is an issue for you, it will be worth checking out this specification.

Hot tip

If you need a monitor suitable for use in brightly lit conditions, models offering a Brightness rating of 500 cd/m2 are available.

...cont'd

Interfaces

Like all other computer devices, monitors need some way of connecting to the system and, to this end, they come with various interfaces.

Currently, the standard interface is DVI (Digital Visual Interface), which has replaced the older analogue VGA (Video Graphics Array) interface and is found on all monitors. However, VGA is still included on many older, and low-end, monitors.

More recent monitors may have an HDMI (High-Definition Multimedia Interface) connector as well as a DVI connector. The purpose of this is to provide a connection for consumer video equipment such as Blu-ray players, TVs, etc. If you don't intend to use your PC for this type of purpose though, a DVI connection is all you'll need.

Another type of interface now being seen on high-end monitors is the DisplayPort interface. This has been developed to eventually replace the DVI interface in IT equipment such as home and office PCs, projectors, monitors, and data center consoles. It provides many advantages over DVI and HDMI, which include:

- The daisy chaining of displays with no loss of performance
- The use of up to 15 meter cables without loss of performance
- Support for multiple monitors on a single connection
- Support for 3D applications
- Low power consumption

Users who will be interested in the DisplayPort interface are gamers, power-users, and those looking to future-proof their system. For general PC use, the DVI interface is perfectly adequate and will be for some time to come.

Discussion of the DisplayPort interface leads us to an interesting monitor development – namely a recently developed technology called Eyefinity.

Eyefinity

Developed by AMD/ATI, Eyefinity is a technology that enables Windows Vista, Windows 7 and Linux 4 operating systems to see multiple display panels as a "Single Large Surface (SLS)", and span video (including 3D) across the panels, thus enabling multiple monitor operation.

Beware

A monitor cannot be connected to the computer via an HDMI connection. For this you will need either a DVI, VGA or DisplayPort connection.

Hot tip

To create an Eyefinity setup, your monitors and video card will need to be DisplayPort compatible.

Two modes are possible with Eyefinity: Duplicated Mode operation (desktop cloned on multiple displays) and Extended Mode (desktop extended across multiple displays). An example of the latter is shown below:

Up to six monitors can be supported by Eyefinity with each one having an independent resolution, refresh rate, and display rotation setting.

The benefits for certain types of user are considerable. With so much screen real estate available, gamers will have greater peripheral vision, spatial awareness, and be able to eliminate blind spots. Throw 3D into the mix and it all adds up to a much more immersive gaming experience.

For professional users who multi-task, Eyefinity optimizes productivity by enabling multiple applications, data sources, etc, to be viewed simultaneously.

Movie buffs can buy specially designed monitors with very thin bezels and use them to create a huge home theatre.

Now for the caveats! An Eyefinity setup is going to cost a serious amount of cash. Not only do you need to buy up to six monitors equipped with a DisplayPort interface, you require one of the latest Eyefinity capable video cards that provides a DisplayPort output.

Don't forget that running all this hardware will require a highly specified PC as well.

On the plus side, all the monitors can be powered by a single video card as long as it has a DisplayPort output.

Hot tip

Nvidia have a similar technology to Eyefinity called 3D Surround. However, Eyefinity is currently the more capable technology.

Installing an LCD Monitor

LCD monitors can be connected to the system via either VGA or DVI connections. However, if it is available, DVI is the best method as some loss of picture quality may occur with the VGA connection.

Monitor connected to a video card DVI port

Monitor connected to a video card VGA port

9 Testing the Basic System

The guts of your new PC are now in place. Hopefully, you haven't made any mistakes so far. If you have, they must be rectified before you proceed further. Here, we show you the likely problems and how to resolve them.

Why Do This Now?

Hot tip

If your motherboard has an integrated video system, you can use this and leave the video card out for the time being. This will be one less potential cause of problems at this stage.

Once the basic system is operational, you can then install the video card and run the test again. If it fails, you'll know immediately that the video card is the source of the problem.

At the moment, your system consists of the power supply unit, motherboard, CPU, memory, video system and monitor (as shown below). This is the minimum required to get a display. Before you go any further you also need to connect the keyboard to the system to provide a means of input.

Having connected the keyboard, if you now test the system and it fails to work you know the problem lies with one of the above devices.

You can, of course, take the optimistic approach and build the system completely by installing all the other parts, such as the hard drive, removable disk drives, and peripherals as well. If it works, fine. However, if it does not, you will then be faced with many more potential causes for the failure. For example, a hard drive that hasn't been connected, or configured, correctly will prevent the computer from booting.

Beware

Don't be tempted to install everything in one go and hope it all works.

Unless you've built computers before, this is not the way to do it.

To keep head scratching to the minimum, you should test each device as you install it (where possible) and make sure it works before moving on to the next. There is nothing wrong with optimism, but a more pragmatic approach may well save you time in the end.

Check the Monitor

It really would be a complete waste of time to troubleshoot a system that seemingly refuses to boot-up, when all along the problem is a malfunctioning or incorrectly adjusted monitor.

Therefore, this is the stage at which you check this device. To help you do it, all modern monitors will display a message or splash screen of some sort when switched on to indicate they are operational. For this to work, however, the monitor must be isolated from the computer, i.e. the signal cable must be disconnected from the video system's output socket.

Check it out as follows:

1. Plug the monitor's power cable into the wall socket. Switch it on, give it a few seconds to warm up and then you should see a test signal similar to the one below

If you don't see a test signal and the monitor lights are off, then either the monitor itself is faulty or it is not getting any power. Check the power supply, plug, and cable. If these are all OK then the monitor must be faulty.

If you do see a light on the monitor, make sure it's not simply in Standby mode. Press the power switch again.

When you do have a working monitor, hook it up to the system as shown on page 100.

as shown on page 100.

Don't forget

Before the monitor will display a test screen, it must be isolated from the computer.

Hot tip

If you are in any doubt about a monitor, another way to test it is by connecting it to a different system.

Hot tip

If you cannot get anything on the monitor, check that the contrast and brightness controls haven't been turned right down inadvertently.

Beware

Monitors carry high voltages that can be lethal. These voltages will remain until discharged. Never open up a monitor for any reason.

Check the Connections

Before you switch your system on for the first time, it may be as well to check all the connections. It is not encouraging to be greeted by a blank screen at the first attempt.

A blank screen is not what you want to see

Don't forget

Do not forget about the power on/off switch at the rear of the power supply unit. Many people never bother looking at the rear of the case and have no idea there is even one there.

Hot tip

One of the most likely things to get wrong is the computer's on/off switch connection to the motherboard. This will be in a row of 2-pin connectors (see page 76) and it is very easy to pick the wrong one.

So, check the following before you do:

- The PC's power cable is plugged into a wall socket
- The switch at the rear of the power supply unit is on
- The monitor is plugged into a wall socket
- The monitor's signal cable is connected to the video system
- The PC's on/off switch is connected to the correct terminals on the motherboard
- The motherboard is connected to the power supply unit
- The memory modules are seated in their sockets and held in place by the retaining clips
- The CPU fan is connected to the motherboard

If everything appears to be OK, the moment of truth has arrived. It's time to switch on and see what happens.

Does it Work?

Having switched on, what you see next depends on the BIOS chip in your system – see margin notes. If your system has an AWARD BIOS, you should see something like the following:

```
     Award Modular BIOS v6.00PC
     Cop                         .rd Software, Inc

     X58A-UD3R FB

     Main Processor : Intel (R) Core(TM) i7 CPU 3.74GHz (178x22)
     <CPUID :000106A5 Patch ID :00000011>
     Memory Testing : 6290432K OK

     Memory Frequency 1360MHz
     Detecting IDE Drives ...
     IDE Channel 0 Master : None
     IDE Channel 1 Master : None
     IDE Channel 2 Master : None
     IDE Channel 3 Master : None


     <Del> :BIOS Setup <F9> :XpressRecovery2 <F12> :Boot Menu <End> Qflasl
     08/24/2010-X58-ICH10-7A89QGONC-00
```

> **Hot tip**
>
> In this chapter you will see several references to the BIOS. This is a chip on the motherboard that carries out a series of routines that starts the computer. These include identifying all the hardware in the system, and checking that they are working correctly.

If you have an AMI BIOS, you should see this or similar:

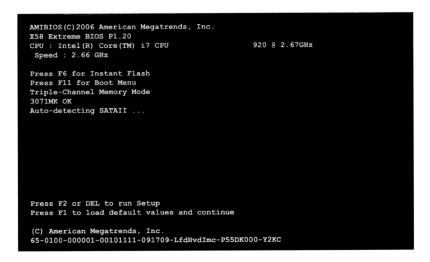

```
AMIBIOS(C)2006 American Megatrends, Inc.
X58 Extreme BIOS P1.20
CPU : Intel(R) Core(TM) i7 CPU        920 @ 2.67GHz
 Speed : 2.66 GHz

Press F6 for Instant Flash
Press F11 for Boot Menu
Triple-Channel Memory Mode
3071MK OK
Auto-detecting SATAII ...




Press F2 or DEL to run Setup
Press F1 to load default values and continue

(C) American Megatrends, Inc.
65-0100-000001-00101111-091709-LfdHvdImc-P55DK000-Y2KC
```

Both displays indicate that you're off to a good start. The fact that you can see text on the screen, and that the boot procedure has completed the memory test, shows that all the components are functioning correctly.

> **Hot tip**
>
> If you have an AWARD BIOS in your system, as the computer boots-up you should hear a long single beep (assuming a speaker is present). This is one of a series of beep codes (see page 108), and indicates that the BIOS has found no problems.
>
> This is not the case with AMI BIOSs, though – a beep indicates a fault. No beep indicates all is well.

...cont'd

The system will continue to boot and then stop with an error message. With an AWARD BIOS you will see this, or similar:

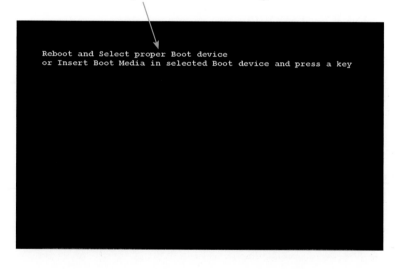

```
                                              L2 Cache Size     :    64K

Diskette Drive A : 1.44M 3.5 in          Display Type       : EGA/VGA
Diskette Drive B : None                  Serial Ports       : 3FB
Pri. Master Disk : None                  Parallel Port(s)   : 378
Pri. Slave Disk  : None                  DDR SDRAM at Bank  : 1
Sec. Master Disk : None
Sec. Slave Disk  : CD-RW  ATA 33


PCI Device Listing ...
Bus No. Device No. Func/No. Vendor/Device Class Device Class              IRQ

     0      16       0      1106  3038   0C03   USB 1.0/1.1 UHCI Cntrlr    11
     0      16       1      1106  3038   0C03   USB 1.0/1.1 UHCI Cntrlr    11
     0      16       2      1106  3038   0C03   USB 1.0/1.1 UHCI Cntrlr     5
     0      16       3      1106  3104   0C03   USB 2.0 UHCI Cntrlr         3
     0      17       1      1106  0571   0101   IDE Cntrlr                 14
     0      17       5      1106  3059   0401   Multimedia Device           5
     1       0       0      1002  5961   0300   Display Cntrlr             11
                                               ACPI Controller             9

Verifying DMI Pool Data .................
Boot from CD :
DISK BOOT FAILURE, INSERT SYSTEM DISK AND PRESS ENTER
```

With an AMI BIOS you will see something like this:

```
    Reboot and Select proper Boot device
    or Insert Boot Media in selected Boot device and press a key
```

Both messages indicate a boot disk error and in this case, it is because the boot disk (hard drive) has not yet been installed.

If the system gets as far as this, then it is working as it should and you can give yourself a pat on the back. The next stages will be installing the hard drive (see pages 123-124) and then installing the operating system (see pages 163-165). If, however, it does not, then go on to the next page.

Hot tip

Boot screens can load so quickly that it may be difficult to get any information from them. However, you can stop them at any time by pressing the Pause key on the keyboard. To resume, press Enter.

The PC Doesn't Boot-Up

Things have not gone as planned. The PC either doesn't boot at all or doesn't reach the boot disk error message stage as shown on page 106. Troubleshoot as follows:

The System is Dead

First, make sure it really is "dead". Check that none of the LEDs on the case or keyboard are lit, the PSU/CPU fans are not running, and that the PC is not making any beeping sounds.

If there are absolutely no signs of life, then you have a power supply fault. Check the following:

- Is there power at the wall socket? Plug another appliance into it. If that works, the PC is getting power

- Check the fuse in the power cable plug

- Is the power cable OK? Try replacing it (many household appliances use the same type)

- Check that the PSU on/off switch at the top-rear of the system case is not in the off position

If these all check out then the power supply unit is defective and will need replacing.

The System is Alive but the Screen is Blank

The system is powered up but there is nothing on the screen – this is the more likely scenario.

A faulty or incorrectly installed motherboard, CPU, memory module or video card can all be the cause of a blank display. Fortunately, when the BIOS finds a major part that is not working, it advises the user accordingly in the form of a series of coded beeps, known not surprisingly as beep codes.

NOTE: a single beep is normal with AWARD BIOSs and indicates that the BIOS has found no problems. You will hear this every time at start-up. This is not the case with AMI BIOSs though – one beep with these indicates a memory problem.

The BIOS chip manufacturers all have their own versions of these codes so you will first need to establish the manufacturer of your BIOS chip. This information will be found in the motherboard manual, and also at the top of the initial boot screen.

Hot tip

Absolutely the first thing to check when your PC appears to be dead is the power supply. Don't forget to check the external AC supply as well.

Hot tip

The easiest way to establish that your power supply unit is operational is to check that its fan is working and that the system case lights are on.

Beep Codes

Having done so, find the code you are hearing in the table below. This may isolate the faulty component.

Beeps	Fault
AWARD BIOS	
1 long, 2 short	Video system
Continuous	Memory
1 long, 3 short	Video system
AMI BIOS	
1	Memory
2	Memory
3	Memory
4	Motherboard
5	CPU
6	Motherboard
7	CPU
8	Video system
9 to 11	Motherboard

Troubleshooting Motherboards

If the beep codes indicate a problem with the motherboard (or you have reason to suspect it), the first thing to check is that the CPU's fan is running. This will confirm that the board is receiving power. If it isn't, check that the fan is connected to its power socket and that the power cable from the PSU is connected to the motherboard (see page 75).

Next, try reseating the CPU in its socket. Do the same with the memory modules even if the beep code is not specific to either.

Check that you haven't dropped something metallic, such as a screw or washer, into the board when installing it. This could create a short-circuit that may prevent it from working.

Do the keyboard LEDs come on? If they don't, the board is almost certainly faulty. If they do, this indicates that the board is active, in which case the problem is more likely to be with the CPU or memory.

Hot tip

The BIOS chip has a built-in diagnostic utility that alerts you to any problems it encounters during boot-up. It does this in two ways – a series of coded beeps if the problem occurs before the video system has initialized, or a text error message (see inside front cover) if the fault comes after.

Hot tip

Before condemning a motherboard, it is always worth checking that the CPU and memory modules are firmly seated in their respective sockets.

There is also the possibility of not hearing any beeps at all. This means nothing with an AMI BIOS but with an AWARD BIOS it is significant.

In the latter case, make sure the case speaker is connected to the correct motherboard terminals. If there are still no beeps, then you definitely have a problem with the motherboard. This will be confirmed if the keyboard and case LEDs are dead as well.

Troubleshooting the Video System

The first thing to check is that the monitor's signal cable is securely connected to the video system's output socket. If your system has both a video card and an integrated system, make sure the monitor is connected to the video card's output socket.

If you are using a PCI-Express video card, make sure you have connected its 4-pin power supply (see page 89). Then reseat the card to make sure the connection is good.

If the screen is still blank, there is one more option open to you, assuming your motherboard has an integrated video system. Switch the computer off and remove the video card from the system. Then connect the monitor cable to the integrated system's video output. Switch on, and if you now have video then you have a faulty video card.

Troubleshooting Memory

If the beep code indicates a memory problem, the first thing to do is make sure the module is fitted correctly (as described on pages 41-42).

Next, install the module into a different slot and try again. It isn't unheard of for a memory socket to be faulty.

If the problem persists then the module is damaged and will need replacing. If you have installed two modules, try removing one of them and restarting. If the PC still doesn't work, replace it with the other one. While it is unlikely, if one of the modules is damaged, it could prevent the other one from working.

Otherwise, replace the module with a new one as you have almost certainly damaged it by careless handling.

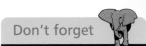

Don't forget

No beeps at all with an AWARD BIOS, assuming the PC has power and the case speaker is correctly connected, is a certain indicator of a motherboard failure.

Don't forget

If you are experiencing video card problems, try removing the card and connecting the video cable to the motherboard's integrated video system (if there is one). If you now get text on the screen, then the video card is faulty and will need replacing.

...cont'd

Boot-up Doesn't Complete

By this we mean the boot procedure starts but doesn't reach the boot disk error message stage, which is as far as it can go without a hard drive and operating system.

Hot tip

If the computer starts to boot and then stops at the memory test, the memory module is either not connected correctly or is faulty.

However, you will at least be seeing text on the screen, which indicates the motherboard, CPU, and video system are all operational. This leaves only the memory as a potential cause of the problem and, in all likelihood, boot-up will stop at the memory test stage, as shown below.

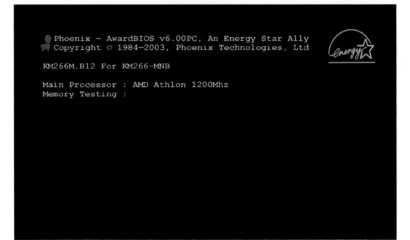

Troubleshoot as described on page 109.

As a general note, assuming the components you are installing are all new, the likelihood of any of them being faulty is very remote. It is far more likely that any problems will be connection issues.

The most common mistakes here are incorrect fitting of the case switches to the motherboard, connecting the monitor to the wrong video system (integrated instead of the video card, or vice versa) and damaging the memory module/s by careless handling.

As a final note, be aware that troubleshooting PC hardware is restricted to identifying and then replacing the faulty board or component. Repairing them is not an option.

10 Hard Drives

In this chapter, you'll learn about the interfaces used by these devices and important specifications – factors that need to be considered when buying a drive. We also look at the various types of hard drive, and the applications for which they are best suited.

Overview

Hot tip

You are well advised to spend your money on a low-capacity drive of high quality, rather than a low-quality drive that has a huge capacity, which in all likelihood you will never use anyway.

The hard drive is where all your data is stored, so if it fails – and when they do, it is almost always terminal – all that data is lost.

Bear in mind, also, that these are mechanical devices (SSD drives excepted) so the one thing you can be certain about is that they will fail eventually.

These two facts make it absolutely critical that you get the best quality hard drive you can afford. This is not a component to cut costs on. Don't even think about budget or second-hand models.

When buying a hard drive you need to consider the following factors:

- Interface – USB, FireWire, SATA, SCSI, SAS, etc
- Type – SSD, Hybrid, external or internal
- Specifications
- Storage capacity
- Intended use of the drive

Interfaces

A hard drive interface is the technology used to connect the drive to the system. There are several drive interfaces, all of which offer different data transfer rates and features. Some are designed for internal drives and some for external drives.

Note that hard drives are classified according to the interface they are designed to use, e.g. a drive that uses the SATA interface is known as a SATA drive.

The issue of data transfer rates can be very confusing for the uninitiated as they are commonly quoted in two different metrics. For example, a FireWire drive is quoted at 800 Mbps, and a SATA drive is quoted at 300 MBps. Which is the faster?

Many people will think it's the FireWire drive and they will be wrong because Mbps is an acronym for Megabits per second, while MBps is an acronym for Megabytes per second. 800 Mbps equates to 100 MBps, so in the example above the SATA drive is three times as fast as the FireWire drive.

In this chapter, we'll be using Megabytes per second (MBps) as this is the metric used by Windows operating systems and so will be the one most familiar to users.

Serial ATA (SATA)

SATA is a development of the PATA (Parallel Advanced Technology Attachment) interface and has now superseded it to become the mainstream internal hard drive interface. Virtually all drives fitted in consumer PCs use this interface.

There are several versions of SATA: The original, SATA 150, has a data transfer rate of 150 MBps, the second, SATA 300, transfers data at 300 MBps, and the third, SATA 600, has a transfer rate of 600 MBps.

Of the three, SATA 300 is currently the de facto version. SATA 600 will eventually take over but at the moment offers a level of performance that very few users need. Also, SATA 600 compatible motherboards are relatively scarce, plus they are more expensive.

To eliminate any confusion, note that the first version of SATA can be denoted as SATA, SATA 150, or SATA 1. The second version as SATA 300, SATA II, or SATA 2. The third version as SATA 600, SATA III or SATA 3.

...cont'd

External SATA (eSATA)

The eSATA interface is basically an extension of SATA and is used to connect external hard drives. Prior to its introduction,

external drives used either FireWire or USB 2, both of which have considerably slower data transfer rates than the SATA 300 interface. eSATA, which operates at the same speed as SATA 300, enables external drives to run at the same speed as an internal SATA hard drive.

Universal Serial Bus (USB)

USB is a system interface that is similar in concept to FireWire. It enables up to 127 devices to run simultaneously on a computer and has many of the features offered by FireWire, such as hot-swapping, plug-and-play and power provision.

As we saw on page 53, USB currently comes in two versions – USB 2, which has a data transfer speed of 57 MBps, and the much faster USB 3, which has a transfer rate of 572 MBps.

Of the two, USB 2 is currently the mainstream standard and will be found on all motherboards built from 2004 onwards. Virtually all the USB devices in current use are designed to use this version.

The recent introduction of USB 3, which is not only ten times as fast as USB 2 but also offers many other technological advances, has probably sounded the death knell for FireWire and eSATA. Not only is it much faster, it does everything FireWire and eSATA do, and more. As a result, new motherboards may soon be offering USB 3 only, as by doing so the manufacturers will be able to cut their costs.

With regard to hard drives, USB is only used by external models.

Hot tip

USB 2 is sometimes referred to as Highspeed USB, and USB 3 is sometimes referred to as Superspeed USB.

Hot tip

USB 3 is some ten times faster than USB 2. So if you decide on a USB hard drive, get one that supports USB 3. Your system probably won't be able to make use of the extra speed but it's pointless buying into yesterday's technology.

FireWire

FireWire (also known as IEEE 1394 and iLink), is a system interface that comes in two versions: FireWire 400, with a data transfer rate of 50 MBps, and FireWire 800, with a transfer rate of 100 MBps.

As with USB and eSATA, this interface is used to connect external devices and, for a considerable period, its characteristics made it the best available interface for this purpose. It was commonly used on video equipment such as camcorders, and external hard drives.

However, with the advent of USB 2, its popularity has waned somewhat. While current external drives still offer it, usually with USB 2 as well, modern video equipment has switched over to USB 2 and HDMI.

Small Computer System Interface (SCSI)

As with USB and FireWire, SCSI is a system interface that is not limited just to disk drives – it can also be used for printers, scanners, etc.

SCSI has been around for a long time now, which is a testament to its capabilities. It is a very fast interface having a maximum data transfer rate of 320 MBps, and is extremely reliable. Also, devices in a SCSI setup can carry out actions without having to involve the main system processor. This reduces system overhead, increases efficiency and results in lower power usage.

These factors, plus others, make it ideally suited for running large numbers of hard drives in corporate and server environments.

Serial Attached SCSI (SAS)

SAS is basically a much improved version of SCSI and offers a data transfer rate of 600 MBps. With this interface, every drive in the system has a dedicated channel, unlike SCSI where all the drives have to share one channel.

SAS interface cables are also narrower than SCSI cables, which makes them easier to route and also improves airflow in the system case.

As with SCSI, the advantages provided by SAS are particularly relevant in business environments.

Don't forget

The SCSI and SAS interfaces are not supported by mainstream motherboards, which means an adapter has to be installed.

Hard Drive Specifications

A suitable interface is just one aspect of buying a hard drive. With so many to choose from, consideration of the following specifications will help narrow the field. Some are important while others are less so. We'll start with the latter:

External Data Transfer Rate

Many buyers get somewhat fixated by External Data Transfer Rate figures believing that the higher the figure, the faster the drive. This is not the case, however; the External Data Transfer Rate specification is the speed at which data is transferred to and from the drive. It is not a measure of drive speed at all but rather the measure of the drive's interface speed (see pages 113-115).

Furthermore, it is not a particularly important specification as the figures quoted are theoretical maximums that can only be reached under ideal operating conditions, which of course, are almost impossible to achieve. Very few users have a PC that can fully utilize the 150 MBps of the now obsolete SATA 150 interface, never mind the 300 and 600 MBps of the SATA 300 and SATA 600 interfaces.

The bottom line therefore, is that for the average user External Data Transfer Rates are not worth worrying about as a PC built with components of just average quality will, by far, exceed their requirements in this respect. It's only to power-users looking to build a super-fast system that it may be relevant.

Internal Data Rate

This specification specifies the speed at which the drive can read and write data from its storage disks and transfer it to the drive's buffer, from where it is sent via the interface to the system.

However, as with External Data Transfer Rates, this specification is largely irrelevant as current drives all have an internal rate that is faster than most modern PCs can utilize. Typical figures for modern drives range from 100 MBps to 300 MBps.

Reliability

Hard drive manufacturers rate their products in terms of longevity with the use of two metrics. The first is Start/Stop Cycles, which is an estimate of how many times a drive can be started and stopped before it fails. Low-end drives are rated at around 50,000 cycles, while those at the high-end are about 600,000 cycles.

Don't forget

As with the External Data Transfer Rate specification, Internal Data Rate specs can be ignored.

The second is MTBF (Mean Time Between Failures). Specified in hours, it is a simple estimate of how long a drive will run before failure occurs. Typical MTBFs for low-end drives are 1,000,000 hours, and 1,500,000 hours for high-end drives.

Our advice is to take these figures with a large pinch of salt, however. They are useful for comparison purposes only.

Rotational (Spindle) Speed

This is the speed at which the drive's motor spindle spins and is a very important specification as it directly affects how quickly data can be transferred to and from the drive's storage disks.

Low-end drives run at 5400 rpm, mainstream drives run at 7200 rpm, and high-end drives run at 10,000-15,000 rpm.

Average Seek Time

Another very important specification, Average Seek Time is a measure of the speed with which the drive can position its read/write heads over a data track. This specification is measured in milliseconds and for low- to mid-range drives, a typical figure is 8-9 ms. High-end drives come in around 3.5 ms.

Buffer Size

A drive's buffer is a small amount of memory built-in to the drive, which is used to store frequently used data. When this data is accessed again, it is read from the much faster buffer memory rather than from the drive's storage disks, thus increasing performance considerably. The larger the buffer, the better the drive's performance.

Buffer size on low-end drives will be 8 MB, mid-range drives 16-32 MB and high-end drives 32-64 MB.

Capacity

How much drive capacity do you need? Take a look at your present system, see how many GBs you have used, and then add on whatever you think you are likely to need in the future.

When you've arrived at a figure, add 30 per cent to it. The reason for doing this is that hard drives only perform efficiently at up to about 70 per cent of their capacity. Any higher than this and data transfer rates start slowing down.

Types of Hard Drive

As with interfaces, there are various types of hard drive. Most of them are named after the interface they use, hence we have SATA, eSATA, SCSI, SAS, USB and FireWire drives.

While the above are all mechanical devices and use the same basic electro-magnetic technology, they each have strengths that make them suitable for specific applications and weaknesses that render them less suitable for others.

A recent development in hard drive technology is Solid State Drives (SSDs). These devices have no moving parts, are compact and rugged, and offer blindingly fast performance.

We'll start with hard drives designed for internal use.

SATA Drives

Internal SATA drives are currently the hard drive of choice for the vast majority of PC owners. While they are not the best type of drive, they offer the most practical storage solution in terms of performance versus cost.

Low-end to mid-range SATA drives use the SATA 300 interface, which provides a very healthy maximum data transfer rate of 300 MBps. Models in this class, typically, have a rotational or spindle speed of 7200 rpm, a buffer size of 8-32 MB, and a seek time of around 8.5 seconds.

In terms of reliability, these drives have a typical rating of 50,000 Stop/Start Cycles, and an MTBF rating of around 1,000,000 hours.

At the high-end of the SATA market, drives use the SATA 600 interface (600 MBps data transfer rate), have a rotational speed of 10,000 rpm, a buffer size of 32-64 MB, and a seek time of 3.5 seconds. The reliability specs are 600,000 Start/Stop cycles and a MTBF of 1,500,000.

SATA hard drives are currently available in capacities of up to 3 TB (3000 GB).

SCSI Drives

SCSI drives have long been the hard drive favored for applications that demand the highest levels of performance and reliability.

Hot tip

If you are not looking for anything out of the ordinary with respect to your hard drive, a SATA 300 model is the obvious choice. It will provide good performance at a sensible price.

This is due to the fact that these drives have an extremely high build quality and are also capable of fast data transfer rates (320 MBps) due to use of the SCSI interface.

SCSI drives have a rotational speed of 15,000 rpm, a buffer size of 16 MB, and a seek time of 3.5 seconds. Reliability figures are 600,000 Start/Stop cycles and a MTBF of 1,500,000.

The drawbacks of SCSI drives are that storage capacity is limited to around 300 GB, and that the high spindle speed makes them considerably more noisy in operation than SATA drives. Also, mainstream motherboards do not provide the SCSI interface, which means that if a user wants to use one of these drives, an SCSI adapter card will have to be installed. This further increases the cost of an already expensive setup.

SAS Drives

SAS drives are essentially the same as SCSI models but the use of the SAS interface enables them to offer improved performance.

Rotational speed, buffer size, seek time, and reliability specifications are much the same as with SCSI drives. However, the SAS interface enables a maximum data transfer rate of up to 600 MBps.

While these drives are also noisy due to the high spindle speeds, and expensive; they do offer much higher storage capacities than SCSI drives of up to 1 TB. Also, as with SCSI drives, a SAS adapter card will have to be installed as mainstream motherboards do not provide the SAS interface.

SSD Drives

Solid state drives are the latest thing to hit the hard drive market. These devices use solid-state memory to store data and contain no moving parts which, quite apart from anything else, makes them extremely reliable.
The key components of an SSD are the memory chips (usually of non-volatile flash memory type), and a processor that acts as a controller.
Incorporated into the controller is the interface that connects the drive to the PC, and this is usually SATA 300 or PCI-Express x4.

Beware

SCSI hard drives have a high rotational speed (typically, 15000 rpm). Side effects of this are higher noise and heat emission levels. Also, maximum storage capacities are less than with SAS and SATA drives.

SSDs offer many advantages over traditional mechanical drives. For example:

- SSDs start instantaneously; HDDs take several seconds

- SSD access time is about 0.1 ms; HDD access time ranges from 3.5 to 10 ms

- SSD read performance is consistent, whereas with HDDs it varies according to the level of drive fragmentation

- SSDs are completely silent in operation as they have no moving parts

- No moving parts makes SSDs almost 100 per cent reliable All HDDs are prone to mechanical and heat issues

- SSDs are much smaller and lighter than HDDs

- SSDs require much less power than HDDs

Beware

A further negative aspect of SSDs is that their performance degrades over time. To combat this, a technology known as TRIM is used and, currently, the only operating system that supports TRIM is Windows 7.

However, there are issues with these devices: One is their cost – an SSD costs about $2.00 per GB while a mechanical hard drive costs about ten cents per GB. That's 20 times as expensive.

Another is that low-end models have a write speed (typically, 50 MBps) that is no better than that of a mechanical hard drive. While their read speed can be as high as 350 MBps, they don't move data any faster than an ordinary HDD. This limitation does not apply to the high-end models though, which have write speeds similar to their read speeds.

SSDs also require a bit more attention during the installation procedure than mechanical drives do. Furthermore, changes need to be made to the operating system's default settings in order to get, and maintain, the best performance from them.

H-HHD Drives

A hybrid hard drive is basically a SATA mechanical drive, which also incorporates a cache (typically 3 or 4 GB in size) of the same type of flash memory used in SSDs.

In operation, frequently used data is stored in the flash memory and because the seek time of flash memory is so fast, when the data is accessed again, the drive's response is almost as fast as that of an SSD.

In operation these drives approach the speed of an SSD while, at the same time, providing much greater, and much cheaper, storage capacity. In terms of overall performance, a modern hybrid drive slots in between high-end 10,000 rpm SATA drives and solid-state drives.

Needless to say, there are drawbacks. A hybrid drive spins-up and spins-down more often than a normal hard drive, which results in greater mechanical wear and tear, and hence a shorter working life. This can also increase noise levels.

It should also be noted that Hybrid drives are designed for use with Laptops and, accordingly, have the 2.5 inch form factor. However, they can be used in a Desktop PC with a suitable mounting bracket.

External Hard Drives

Hard drives designed to be used externally come in two types – Desktop with a 3.5 inch form factor, and Portable with a 2.5 inch form factor. Both types use the same SATA technology found in mainstream SATA internal drives.

The only differences are that external models are supplied in a protective case or enclosure, and that some need a seperate power supply.

As regards interfaces, most of them use both USB 2 (recent models USB 3), and FireWire 800, while others use eSATA.

Currently, the highest capacity for a single drive is 3 TB. However, for those who need even more storage than this, external drive enclosures are available with two, or more, 3 TB drives configured in a RAID 0 setup for increased performance.

Hot tip

External hard drives come pre-partitioned and formatted. Simply plug them in and they're ready to go.

Hot tip

External drives are available in "tough case" models that are built to withstand being dropped and otherwise physically abused.

121

Buying a Hard Drive

By now you should have a good idea of what to look for when buying a drive for your new system. If you're still unsure, however, the following may help:

Of all the components in a computer system, the one that most needs to be of high quality is the hard drive because this is where all a user's data is kept. While even low-end drives provide a performance level that is more than adequate for most users, their build quality, and hence reliability, are not acceptable when mission-critical data needs to be stored. In this type of environment, the choice has to be an SCSI or SAS drive. This will be expensive though as both of these drives require an adapter card to be fitted, and these can be as expensive as the drive itself.

The intended use of the PC also has a big bearing on the choice of hard drive. Applications such as gaming, video, CAD, etc, all require a highly specified PC. Putting a low-end drive into such a system will effectively drag all the high quality components down to its level. To get the best out of these types of application, a SATA 600 drive with a spindle speed of 10,000 rpm, or an SSD will be necessary. For more general, less demanding use, a SATA 300 drive will be fine.

Don't get too bogged down with hard drive specifications. These can be misleading (sometimes deliberately so) and in many cases lead buyers into assumptions that are incorrect. Be aware that the drive manufacturers use specification sheets as marketing tools, and the figures they quote are invariably taken under ideal operating conditions that can never be achieved in practice.

Many users have steered clear of external hard drives in the past as they have traditionally been much slower than internal models. This is no longer the case, however, as drives using the eSATA and USB 3 interfaces are every bit as fast. While you will need an internal drive for the operating system and your applications, an external drive as well is ideal for extra storage, and more importantly, as an independent backup medium.

If performance and/or reliability are important but you can't afford a high-end SAS/SCSI drive, consider buying two mid-range drives and setting them up in a RAID 0 (performance) or RAID 1 (reliability) configuration. We explain how to do this on page 162.

Hot tip

RAID is a way of configuring a combination of hard drives to gain specific benefits. Depending on the RAID configuration chosen, these can be performance, reliability, or both.

Installing a Hard Drive

As the vast majority of users will buy a SATA drive, this is what we'll use here to demonstrate the installation procedure.

At the front of the case, you'll see the drive cages. The wider cage at the top is for your CD/DVD drive; the narrower cage below is where the hard drive goes.

In low-end cases, the drive will probably have to be secured by four screws. Better cases usually provide a tool-free method of securing the drive. Whichever, having done so, connect it to the system as shown below:

Hot tip

If you are fitting two or more hard drives, it is advisable to leave a space between the drives to prevent them overheating.

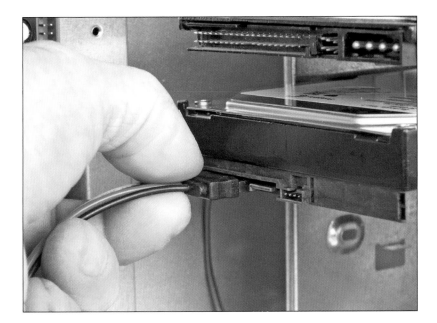

1 Take a SATA power connector from the Power Supply Unit and connect it to the drive's power socket. This is situated at the rear-left of the drive

If your Power Supply Unit does not provide SATA power connectors (likely if you are reusing an older model), you can buy adapters that convert the Molex power connector found in older models into SATA.

...cont'd

 2 Connect one end of the interface cable to the socket at the right of the power supply socket

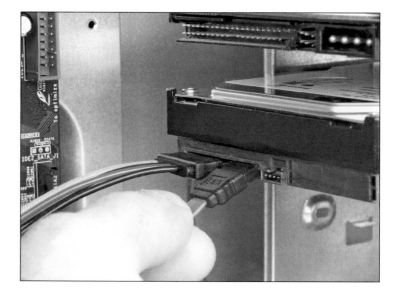

3 Connect the other end to a SATA socket on the motherboard

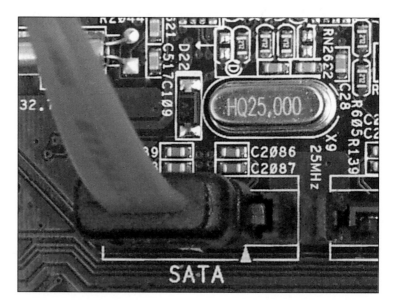

11 Input Devices

In this chapter, we look at the ubiquitous mouse and the keyboard. These are very simple devices which, nevertheless, can provide some very useful features.

Mouse Technology

Optical (LED)

These devices use an LED that projects light onto the work surface. Reflections of the light are picked up by an electronic sensor and translated by a chip into the data needed for positioning the pointer.

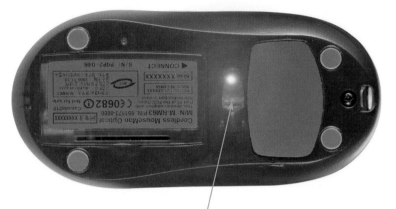

LED and electronic sensor on the underside of the mouse

The advantages of optical technology are: quicker and more precise operation, no moving parts to wear out and the ability to use the mouse on a range of surfaces without the need for a mousemat.

The disadvantages are that they cost a little more and require the use of batteries, which further adds to their cost in the long term.

The majority of today's mice are of the LED type.

Optical (Laser)

These mice have taken optical technology a step further by using a laser as the light source. This is able to read far more data, which together with other technical enhancements, results in a mouse that offers the highest levels of performance. Also, these devices can be used on any type of surface.

Accordingly, laser technology is found only in professional mice intended for use by gamers, and high-end graphic applications. Not surprisingly, they are the most expensive type.

The MX 1000 laser mouse from Logitech

Types of Mouse

Wired

This is the traditional type of mouse and it uses a cord to connect to the PC. The advantage it has over its wireless cousins is that the cord provides a faster and more reliable method of connection

(although it must be said that there is not much in it, particularly in comparison to the high-performance laser mice).

Wireless

Wireless, or cordless, mice use radio frequency (RF) technology as the means of connecting to the PC. This does away with the need for a connecting cord and is their only real advantage.

Their main disadvantage is that a radio frequency connection can introduce a time lag between the user moving the mouse and movement of the pointer.

However, this delay is minute and should only be of concern to professional users (this is why many gamers will only use a wired mouse).

Trackball

A trackball is simply an up-ended version of the old ball and wheel mouse. In operation, the user positions the pointer by rotating the ball with a finger rather than moving the mouse around the desktop.

This makes them ideal for those with hand or wrist disabilities, as they can be operated with a single finger.

Other advantages are that they can be used on any type of surface as the ball doesn't come into contact with it, and they can be used in very confined spaces.

Beware

Make sure that your mouse uses FastRF wireless technology to minimize time lag. Standard RF technology is not so good in this respect. Also, be aware that even FastRF is only effective at up to six feet from the PC. Use the mouse at a greater distance than this and time lag may be introduced.

Mouse Specifications

As with all computer devices, the quality of a mouse is determined by its specifications. However, unlike most PC devices, for the vast majority of users, investigating them really isn't necessary as literally all the mice currently on the market are good enough for all but the most demanding applications.

The only ones who will need to do this are gamers and users of high-end graphic programs.

For those where only the best will do, the following specifications are the ones to be considered:

Tracking Resolution
Tracking is defined as movement, and tracking resolution is the number of pixels that an optical sensor is able to recognize when the device is moved.

The higher the resolution, the more sensitive the mouse and thus, the less movement needed to obtain a response. Standard mice have a resolution of 400 to 800 dpi, while professional models will be up to 5000 dpi.

Tracking Speed
Tracking speed is the maximum speed that the mouse can be moved while still providing accurate tracking. Look for 40 inches per second with standard mice and 65 inches per second with professional mice.

Image Processing Rate
This is a measure of how many mega-pixels of data a mouse can assimilate in a second, and determines its accuracy. The more data the mouse has, the more accurately it can position the pointer. Typical figures range from around 4.7 mega-pixels/sec for standard mice and up to 6.4 for professional models.

Acceleration
Mouse acceleration is how quickly the mouse responds to movement. Standard mice have figures of around 10 g (gravities), while professional mice can be as fast as 30 g.

Don't forget

Unless you are in the market for a high-performance device or have a particular requirement, such as operating distance, mouse specifications as detailed on this page are not something you need to be overly concerned with.

Mouse Features

To enable the user to get the best out of a mouse, it must provide suitable features and controls, particularly if it is designed for professional use. The following are what you should be looking for.

Programmable Buttons
These allow users to map different functions to a button, such as close, open, zoom, etc and allow them to do much more with the mouse.

Basic mice will come with one left-click button, one right-click button and a center scroll wheel, which may also double as a programmable button. Better models will have three or four programmable buttons, while professional models will have up to eight. Professional mice may also have a tilting scroll wheel, which enables horizontal scrolling.

Batteries
A well used optical mouse will go through batteries at a surprising rate, thus adding considerably to its initial cost. Using rechargeables is the best way to minimize this, but good ones are expensive.

Cheap mice will be provided with either no batteries at all, or two standard AA batteries. Factor in the cost of four rechargeables (two in use, two recharging) and the mouse is no longer cheap. So look for a model that provides rechargeables in the box – four, ideally.

Also, consider the type of rechargeables supplied (or bought). Standard nickel cadmium batteries (Ni-Cad) do not last nearly as long as high-capacity Nickel-Metal Hydride (Ni-MH) batteries.

Professional models come with a built-in battery pack and a charging station (shown right), into which you place the device when it's not in use. This keeps it fully charged at all times. A battery life LED indicator is a useful feature to look out for.

Software
Most mice these days come with control panel software that allows you to configure basic functions, such as pointer options, button mapping, etc. The software supplied with better models provide many more options that allow you to customize the mouse to suit particular applications. Some high-end mice allow you to change some settings, e.g. screen resolution, at the click of a button (handy for gamers).

Optical mice, typically, have an operating range of about six feet, which allows you to sit further back from the display.

If you need more than this, consider going for a Bluetooth mouse. This provides an operating range of 30 feet or more (you will of course have to add a Bluetooth adapter to the PC).

Keyboard Technology

Keyboards are simple devices that basically comprise a switching system, LED lights, and a processor to convert the keystrokes to signals that can be interpreted by the PC.

As all types of keyboard have lights and a processor, the main differentiating factor between them is the switching technology used. The most common types are discussed below.

Capacitive

In a capacitive keyboard, each key has its own circuit. When the key is depressed, the capacitance (electrical charge) in the circuit is altered. The change is then translated by the processor. Essentially, it is a non-mechanical system and, as a result, it is the most durable type of keyboard. These devices also have an extremely tactile key action.

Note that capacitive keyboards are very expensive and will be available only from specialist manufacturers.

Mechanical

Next in terms of quality is the mechanical type of keyboard. These devices use a mechanical switch for each key. They also employ a feedback mechanism that produces a tactile "clicky" feel to the key action. In addition, the switches are usually of the self-cleaning variety, which means that they provide good long-term performance.

As with the capacitive type, these keyboards are not commonly available, so you may need to visit a specialist manufacturer.

Membrane

In a membrane keyboard, none of the keys has an individual switch or circuit; instead, they all sit on a sheet of plastic (the membrane). This is imprinted with a metallic pattern that when touched by a depressed key, acts like a switch and sends the "key depressed" signal to the computer.

These keyboards are much cheaper as they have fewer parts inside them. However, they do have the disadvantages of poor durability, and a spongy, non-tactile feel to the key action.

The standard keyboards supplied with PC systems and by PC parts vendors are of the membrane type.

Don't forget

Capacitive and mechanical keyboards are the best choice for professional use. Membrane models are fine for general purpose use.

130

Beware

Touch typists will not get on with a membrane keyboard – their key action is not positive enough.

Types of Keyboard

Rather than settle for the cheap keyboards typically supplied by PC manufacturers, the self-builder has a range to choose from, many of which are designed with specific purposes in mind.

Professional
High-quality keyboards use either a mechanical or capacitive key system as opposed to the membrane system used by cheaper models. For touch typists, they are the best option by far.

Ergonomic
Also intended for the serious typist are the ergonomically designed keyboards. While these take a bit of getting used to, they do make typing a more speedy and comfortable process.

They are constructed in a way that allows users to hold their hands in a more comfortable, slightly angled, position while typing. This can also help prevent or alleviate Carpal Tunnel Syndrome; an affliction that affects the wrists.

Taking the concept a bit further are split keyboards that have an adjustable hinge in the middle to vary the angle at which the keys are presented to the user's hands.

Program Specific
Some keyboards provide keys that are relevant to specific applications. For example, those of you who frequently use Microsoft Office applications can buy models that have keys relevant to Word, PowerPoint, Excel, etc.

Image reprinted with permission from ViewSonic Corporation

Others have keys that control multimedia functions such as play and pause, Internet and email functions.

Hot tip

Also available for serious typists is the Dvorak keyboard. These use a different key layout that is considered to be more efficient than the QWERTY layout found on standard keyboards.

131

Hot tip

Those of you always on the move might like to take their keyboard with them. This is easy with a roll-up keyboard. Made of a thin pliant material such as silicon, you simply roll it up and stuff it in a bag. These devices are very thin and weigh only a few ounces.

...cont'd

Gaming Keyboards

For some game genres, keyboards are the best type of controller, e.g. strategy games, such as Microsoft's Age of Empires, where the game action is controlled by the keyboard.

While standard keyboards are adequate, much better results will be had from one of the specialized gaming keyboards.

These have a multitude of programmable keys and allows the user to customize them to suit specific games. Most also have an integral joystick, plus illuminated keys that allow games to be played in the dark (hardly essential, but cool nevertheless).

One of the most important features that they offer to gamers, is the ability to set up macro commands that combine multiple keystrokes into one. For example, with a standard keyboard, getting a game character to jump forward and kick-out simultaneously will require three keys to be pressed at the same time. A gaming keyboard will do this with one keystroke.

You can also find keyboards tailored for specific games. Take a look at www.steelseries. com. Here you will find a range of keyboards

designed for use with games such as Starcraft 2, Medal of Honor and Cataclysm.

Wireless Keyboards

These are becoming increasingly popular as they reduce the amount of clutter on the desktop. They also enable the user to sit a lot further back from the monitor, thus reducing eyestrain.

These keyboards are more expensive than standard models, though.

Keyboard Specifications

Important keyboard specifications include:

Switching Technology
There are quite a few methods used but the most common are capacitive, mechanical and membrane, as explained on page 130.

Users who do a lot of intensive typing should look at capacitive and mechanical models. All other users will be fine with the membrane type.

Keystrokes
This specification relates to the expected lifespan of the switching technology used by a keyboard.

Capacitive types offer the highest rating – 20 to 50 million keystrokes, while mechanical switching ratings are, typically, around the 20 million mark. Membrane switching is the least durable and varies from 5 to 10 million keystrokes.

Note that a few high-end membrane keyboards offer a keystroke rating of up to 50 million. However, while they may be as durable, they will not be as pleasant to use as capacitive and mechanical types.

Interface
Nearly all keyboards these days use the USB interface. However, it is a fact that the traditional PS/2 keyboard interface is still perfectly adequate for the low bandwidth requirements of any current keyboard.

Therefore, those of you who would rather keep your USB ports for other devices that will benefit from the higher speed USB offers, should consider getting a keyboard that uses the PS/2 port. Note that some keyboards can run from either and will be supplied with a USB to PS/2 adapter.

If you go for a wireless model, be aware of the issue of time lag as explained on page 127; this applies equally to keyboards. Go for one that uses FastRF technology.

Peak Tactile Force
This is the measure of how tactile the key action is and a good figure is 60 to 70 grams.

Hot tip

A keyboard technology exists that employs laser beams to create a virtual keyboard. A device about the size of a cigarette lighter attaches to the PC and projects an image of a full-sized keyboard onto the work surface. It also provides realistic keystroke sounds.

Keyboard Features

As with the mouse, a basic keyboard is functional but will provide nothing in the way of extras. A more fully-featured model can enhance your work in a number of ways. Lets look at some useful examples:

Key Functions

Many keyboards come with a small software program that allows the user to map specific functions to certain keys (usually the F keys). This provides very useful shortcuts that can open web pages and applications with a single keystroke.

Spill Resistance

As many users will testify, it's all too easy to knock a drink over and into the keyboard. Even if this does no permanent damage, in the case of sugary beverages, it may be necessary to remove the key caps to clean away the sticky residue.

Much easier then, to buy a model that is spill resistant. These are designed in such a way that liquids simply pass through the keyboard and can then be drained away through holes at the bottom of the case.

Ergonomic Adjustments

Extended periods of keyboard use can be very tiring on the wrists and fingers and can lead to repetitive stress injuries. Avoid the potential for this by buying a model that features an adjustable typing angle and wrist rest.

Lighting

Backlit keys will be useful when typing in low-light conditions. It can also be an aesthetic feature.

Integrated Pointing Devices

Compactly designed keyboards are available that feature a built-in trackball mouse or touch pad. These keyboards are useful when working in cramped conditions that do not allow enough room for using a separate mouse.

Hot tip

Cheap keyboards have the characters printed on the keycaps and eventually they will wear off. Look for a model that has the characters etched on to the keys.

12 Sound Systems

For most users, integrated sound is quite adequate; we look at the reasons for this. Other users, however, such as gamers and musicians, will need a dedicated sound card. Read on to see why.

Overview

Sound is one of the less important aspects of a computer, as for most tasks, it simply isn't needed. That said, there are probably very few people who would opt to do without it completely as it does add another element to computing. For gamers it is essential.

For the self-builder working to a budget, the computer's sound system offers an opportunity to cut costs. Unless there is a specific need for any of the features provided by a dedicated sound card, an integrated sound system will fit the bill nicely.

Beware

When buying a high-quality sound card, you will also need to factor in the price of a set of high-quality speakers. These can cost as much as the card itself, and so the setup as a whole can turn out to be very expensive.

Most people find the sound systems integrated into the majority of motherboards to be more than adequate for all their sound requirements.

For those who want high-quality sound reproduction, or musicians who need music-mastering facilities, the issue is more complicated, as a top-end sound card will be required. These come with bewildering sets of specifications, features and sockets, and require a bit of homework to ensure the correct choice is made.

For the self-builder who is working to a budget, the high cost of top-end sound cards also needs to be considered as these can cost even more than video cards.

However, for most people, a computer's sound system is an area in which economies can be made with very little penalty in terms of functionality or performance.

Integrated Sound Systems

In the past, the vast majority of computers were supplied with two nasty little speakers, which were good for reproducing the operating system's clicks and jingles, but little else. The integrated sound systems supplied with these PCs were equally basic.

The situation is rather different today, and most of the motherboards currently on the market come with quite sophisticated sound systems that can be good enough even for the gamer.

It is quite common now to find motherboards offering 7.1 high-definition surround sound (and even 9.1 in high-end boards) that can take advantage of multi-speaker setups.

Integrated sound systems do not require the use of a motherboard expansion socket as do sound cards. This gives you more room for expansion in other areas.

One drawback is that they rely on the PC's CPU and memory to do the number-crunching, thus reducing system performance. In addition, they provide less in the way of input and output sockets than sound cards do, which can be restrictive.

Also, good as they are now, they still do not provide the kind of high-fidelity required by the music purist, nor do they offer anything to the musician in the way of authoring features.

If you do decide to take the integrated route, take a look at the specifications as there are still systems around which are not so good. Basically, the more features offered, the better the performance will be.

Features to look for include:

- DirectX (current version 11)
- EAX (current version 5)
- DirectSound 3D
- Open AL
- Input and output ports

Don't forget

As with integrated video, integrated sound systems have their pros and cons.

Advantages are:
- No cost
- No expansion slot used
- No hardware to be installed

Disadvantages are:
- Slight degradation of system performance
- Performance levels, while adequate, do not match those offered by dedicated sound cards
- Limited features
- Limited input & output sockets

Hot tip

If you intend to use a multi-channel integrated sound system, check that the motherboard provides the necessary output sockets – not all do.

Sound Cards

People who need to buy a dedicated sound card will fall into one of the following categories:

- Speed aficionados who don't want to sacrifice even the small hit in performance that integrated sound will make on their system

- Musicians who need specific mastering functions such as Wave Table Synthesis support

- Gamers who want to get the maximum sound effects from their games

- Music buffs who require the highest possible quality of audio reproduction

Budget Sound Cards

If you are looking to make your system as fast as possible, then integrated sound is out due to the demands it makes on the system's CPU and memory. While the drop in performance is relatively slight, it is, nevertheless, there.

In this situation, a low- to mid-level sound card should suffice, as all you are looking for is something to take the load off the CPU and system memory. Anything else it offers is a bonus.

However, you should be aware that some of the really low-end cards actually pass the number-crunching on to the system's CPU, which means that essentially they are no better than integrated sound systems. About the only benefit you may get from one of these cards is better connectivity by way of the number of input and output ports. So check the specifications.

As a general rule, we would advise you not to bother with budget sound cards at all. As already mentioned, very often they are no better than integrated systems; they may, in fact, be even less capable.

Spend a bit more to get a mid-range card, such as the Creative SoundBlaster X-Fi Xtreme Gamer (shown right).

Hot tip

One of the best known manufacturers of sound cards is Creative Labs. They can be found at www.creative.com.

Beware

Some low-end sound cards actually use the system's CPU to do the number-crunching. So if you are looking at the bottom end of the market, study the specifications carefully.

138

Sound Cards for Gamers

Gamers who are not satisfied with the quality of integrated sound need to look at several aspects of sound cards before buying one.

The first point to note is that the fidelity of a sound card's output will be of less importance to the gamer than its ability to create the illusion of being in the middle of the action. For example, if a game character walks behind you, his footsteps should sound as though they are coming from over your shoulder.

To be able to do this, the sound card must provide the following:

- Multiple speaker support – each pair of speakers requires a line-out socket. So a five- or six-speaker system will require three of these, and a seven- or eight-speaker system will require four

- 3D Surround Sound – also known as Positional Audio, this technology accurately recreates the relative positioning of sound in a three-dimensional environment. There are various versions, but the de facto standard is currently Creative's EAX

Also important is the number of simultaneous sounds the card can process (these are referred to as channels [see margin note] in the specifications). If the application throws more of these at the sound card than it is designed to handle, the system's CPU has to help out. If this happens when playing a game, the game's frame rate may be adversely affected.

Thirty-two channels is a reasonable starting point; anything higher is good.

The more APIs (application program interfaces) the card supports, the better. These allow the game to communicate with the sound card, and different types of sound use specific APIs. If they are not supported by the card then you will be missing out on some of the game's sound effects.

The gamer might also want to look at the specifications that determine the fidelity of the sound card's output. Having just saved the world from marauding aliens, he may need to chill-out by listening to a nice piano concerto.

Hot tip

DirectX support is just as important for a sound card as it is for a video card. Make sure the card supports the latest version.

Hot tip

When applied to a sound card, the term "channel" has two meanings:

1) The number of speakers that can be connected to the card. A card with one output jack will be able to support two channels; each channel supporting one speaker – one left, one right. If it has two jacks, it will support four speakers, and so on

2) The number of simultaneous sounds the card can process by itself

...cont'd

High-Fidelity Sound Cards

Music buffs who like to listen to crystal clear audio need to investigate a different set of specifications. 3D Surround Sound will be less important than the fidelity of the sound card's output.

This is indicated by the following specifications:

- Bit-Depth – this indicates how much of the original sound file is reproduced by the card. High bit-depth means high-fidelity and dynamic range

- Signal-to-Noise Ratio (SNR) – this is a measure of how "clean" a sound signal is. The higher the amount of background noise (electrical interference, etc), the lower the signal-to-noise ratio

- Total Harmonic Distortion (THD) – this is a measurement of the amount of unwanted harmonic frequencies that are added to the fundamental frequencies when an audio signal passes through an electronic component

- Frequency Response (FR) – this is the range of frequencies that the sound card can recognise and is specified in upper and lower limits

- Sampling Rate (SR) – this determines the range of frequencies that can be converted to digital format by the sound card, and thus the accuracy of the reproduction

Taken as a whole, these five specifications are the measure of a sound card's output quality.

The figures in the table below show what to expect from low-end, mid-range and top-end sound cards.

	Low-End	Mid-Range	Top-End
Bit-Depth	16-bits	16-bits	24-bits
SNR	75 Db	90 Db	120 Db
THD	0.5 %	0.05 %	0.001 %
FR	20 Hz-20 KHz	20 Hz-20 KHz	10 Hz-22 KHz
SR	48 KHz	48 KHz	96 KHz

Sound Cards For Musicians

In addition to the specifications discussed on page 140, those interested in creating music on their PCs also need to consider the features provided by the card.

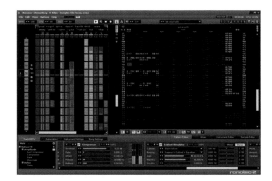

These will include balanced analog inputs/outputs, digital inputs/outputs in AES/EBU or S/PDIF formats, full duplex and dedicated wave-mixers.

Used in conjunction with a suitable mastering application, such as Steinberg's Cubase, a card offering these features will turn a PC into a very capable recording studio.

Whatever type of card you go for, be aware that these devices are prone to picking up electrical interference (noise) from other parts in the system. This manifests itself as humming, hissing, clicks, etc. While good quality sound cards include circuitry to minimize this, it is unlikely to be eliminated completely.

So if you want as clean a signal as possible, buy a card that includes a break-out box as shown below. This either sits on the desktop or can be installed in a spare drive bay, and houses the input/output jacks and the audio converters.

This type of arrangement eliminates the issue of electrical noise by converting the analog signal to digital form *before* it is sent to the card in the PC where noise will be induced from nearby parts, such as the hard drive and other expansion cards.

Hot tip

Do not overlook the "connectivity" of the sound card. The more inputs and outputs it has, the more you will be able to do with it, e.g. microphone recording, the attachment of multiple-speaker systems, digital audio devices and other electronic equipment such as a stereo system.

Don't forget

For high-quality sound output look for a sound card that is supplied with a separate break-out box.

Installing a Sound Card

Install the sound card as you would any other expansion card. However, don't forget the issue of electrical interference from other system devices, as explained on page 141.

If your card is supplied with a break-out box, this will not be a problem. If it's not, minimize interference as much as possible by situating the card as far from other devices as you can. This is demonstrated below.

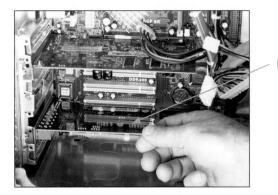

1 Sound card fitted well away from other devices

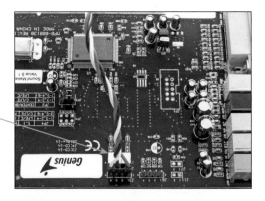

2 Connect the audio cable from the CD/DVD drive (if necessary)

Don't forget

Don't forget to connect the 4-pin analog cable to the CD/DVD drive (if there is one).

3 Secure the backplate to the chassis

13 Removable Media Drives

One of the biggest boons for PC users in recent years has been the introduction of writable disc media. Here we show you what is available, explain the various disc formats, and relevant specifications.

What's Available?

Given the enormous storage capacities offered by today's removable media drives, no self-respecting system can possibly be without one. Their uses are endless – movie and music recording, system backups, data transfer between PCs, etc. The problem is choosing the right type of drive.

Do you settle for a DVD drive or do you splash out for a Blu-ray drive? If you do buy a DVD model, which type do you go for – DVD-ROM, DVD writer or DVD-RAM.

Tape drives, which use cartridges, are ideal for large data backups, but do have disadvantages, the main one being the cost of these devices. A more recent, and cheaper, option is a system that uses hard drives as the removable media – these are known as RDX drives.

Then there is the ubiquitous USB flash drive – cheap and cheerful and handy for any number of purposes. Can you tell a good one from a bad one, though?

Your choices are:

- DVD drives
- Blu-ray drives
- RDX drives
- Tape drives
- USB flash drives

We'll start with the most common type of removable media drive – the DVD drive.

Hot tip

Used in conjunction with a suitable backup utility, high-capacity DVDs enable you to make a complete backup of your system.

DVD Drives

DVD (Digital Versatile Disc) drives are very similar in concept to the old and now discontinued CD drives. The basic difference is that DVD drives use a much narrower laser beam for reading and writing, which enables more tracks to be squeezed onto the discs. This vastly increases their storage capacity.

In addition, the composition of a DVD disc allows two layers of data on each side, giving a theoretical maximum of some 17 GB. In practice though, most DVD discs currently on sale have a capacity of 4.7 GB, with 8.5 GB (dual-layer) versions also available at a higher price.

Due to their high storage capacity, DVD discs are used for commercially produced movies, as an entire movie can be stored on one disc. This capacity is also utilized by the PC industry. For example, Microsoft's Encarta Reference Library, which would require five CDs, is available on a single DVD.

The high capacity of DVD discs is handy for PC users as well. Typical applications are system backups and the storage of video, such as TV shows recorded via TV tuner devices.

Another plus for these drives is the fact that they can also read CDs (both software CDs and writable CDs).

DVD drives are available in three versions: read-only (DVD-ROM), writable (DVD-R) and re-writable (DVD-RW).

DVD Formats

The issue of DVD formats also needs to be considered. Currently, there are four of these.

DVD-ROM

Similar to a CD-ROM, discs in this format can only be read – they cannot be written to.

DVD-

This format is supported by Panasonic, Toshiba, Apple, Hitachi, NEC, Pioneer, Samsung and Sharp. It is available in write-once versions (DVD-R) and rewrite versions (DVD-RW).

DVD+

DVD+ is supported by Philips, Sony, Hewlett-Packard, Dell, Ricoh and others. As with DVD-, write-once (DVD+R) and rewrite (DVD+RW) versions are available.

DVD-RAM

A DVD-RAM disc is very similar to a hard drive in operation. This format also offers faster data access, and higher levels of reliability than the + and - formats. However, DVD-RAM discs can be read only in a DVD-RAM drive – the format is not generally compatible with DVD+ and DVD- drives.

The table below summarizes the pros and cons of the formats:

Disc	Uses	Pros	Cons
DVD-ROM	Commercial movies, PC games, software	Plays on all drives	Cannot be recorded to
DVD-RAM	Data backup	Offers hard drive like operation, and fast data access. Most reliable format	Poor compatibility. Cannot be played on home DVD players. Discs are expensive
DVD-	Good for video and audio discs, general data backup and transfer	High level of compatibility with other formats and home DVD players	Lower maximum capacity than DVD+ discs. Write/read speeds are slower than DVD+
DVD+	Good for mixed data discs. Can also be used for video and audio discs	Good level of compatibility with home DVD players	Compatibility with other formats and home DVD players less than DVD-

Hot tip

If your primary purpose for buying a DVD drive is long-term data storage, consider one of the DVD-RAM drives. DVD-RAM discs have the highest life expectancy of all the formats. Furthermore, the drives themselves provide data protection facilities, e.g. the marking of bad sectors. These features make DVD-RAM the most reliable format.

Don't forget

The DVD+ format is more advanced than DVD-. It offers faster write speeds, slightly higher disc capacity, and built-in data correction. However, the format is generally considered to be less compatible with home and car DVD players.

DVD Drive Specifications

Having decided what type of drive/format you want, the next step is to take a closer look at these devices and see what they actually offer. The following specifications are the ones that should be considered.

Interface

The vast majority of drives currently on the market use the SATA interface. They are also available with USB, FireWire, and SCSI interfaces.

Read/Write Speeds

The speed at which a drive reads and writes is indicated by x ratings in the specifications. Usually, these are marked prominently on the packaging, as shown below.

Better quality DVD drives have a typical read speed of 16x, and a write speed of 24x. With low-end models, the figures are about 12x and 8x respectively. Note that when writing to dual-layer discs, and re-writable discs, write speeds are lower.

DVD drives can also read, and write to, CDs. Typical figures for this type of media are read speeds of 48x and write speeds of 40x.

However, for these figures to have any meaning, you need to know what the x represents. In the case of CDs, it represents 150 KBps. So a CD write speed of 40x means that data is written to the disc at a speed of 6.0 MBps (150 x 40).

In the case of DVDs, the x figure represents 1.32 MBps. So a drive writing a DVD at 22x can write data at a rate of 29 MBps.

With Blu-ray drives, the x represents 6.74 MBps, which means a Blu-ray disc written at 12x will have a write speed of 80 MBps.

Hot tip

The interface used by the drive is something that you don't need to worry about unless you are looking to "future-proof" your system. Both the ATA and the newer SATA interfaces, are more than capable of running any the drives currently on the market at their full potential.

...cont'd

Writing Mode

A very important factor in the performance of an optical drive is the maintenance of a constant data transfer rate across the entire disc. To achieve this, manufacturers use one of three methods: Constant Linear Velocity (CLV), Zoned Constant Linear Velocity (ZCLV) and Constant Angular Velocity (CAV).

All you need to know here is that budget and mid-range drives use the CLV or ZCLV method, while top-end models use CAV.

Access Time

This is the time needed to locate a specific item of data on the disc. This metric is measured in milliseconds and you should look for a figure no higher than 160 ms (DVDs) and 140 ms (CDs).

Buffer Size

Optical drives use a buffer to ensure that data flows to the disc smoothly and without interruption during the writing process; this helps to eliminate errors. Typically, drives are supplied with a 2 MB buffer and this is the minimum that you should accept. High-quality drives can have buffers as large as 8 MB.

Recommended Media

The build quality of CDs and DVDs varies widely and some drives have trouble with low-quality discs. To enable users to avoid this potential problem, most manufacturers provide a list of media recommended for use with their drives, as shown below:

Recommended Media		(All DVD-RW and CD-RW media is rewritable up to 1,000 times)
DVD+R	16X	Taiyo Yuden, Verbatim/Mitsubishi
	8X, 4X	Maxell, Ricoh, Taiyo Yuden, Verbatim/Mitsubishi
DVD+RW	4X	Ricoh, Verbatim/Mitsubishi
DVD+R DL	8X, 4X	Verbatim/Mitsubishi
DVD-R	16X, 8X, 4X	Maxell, Taiyo Yuden, TDK, Verbatim/Mitsubishi
DVD-RW	4X, 2X	TDK, Verbatim/Mitsubishi
DVD-R DL	4X	Verbatim/Mitsubishi, Victor
CD-R	48X	Maxell, Taiyo Yuden, TDK
	40X	Ricoh
CD-RW	32X, 24X	Verbatim/Mitsubishi
	10X, 4X	Ricoh, Verbatim/Mitsubishi Chemical

Dual-Layer Discs

A dual-layer disc stores data on both sides, which doubles the maximum storage capacity of a DVD to 8.5 GB. However, these discs can only be written and read by a dual-layer drive. Also, they currently cost more than twice as much as a single-layer DVD, which makes them poor value for money.

Beware

If you are tempted by the high storage capacities offered by dual-layer DVDs, remember that they will be an expensive way of archiving your data.

Blu-ray Drives

Blu-ray drives are most commonly used in consumer electronic devices, such as stand-alone players and games consoles. However, they are also available in the 5.25 inch form factor, which enables them to be internally installed in a computer.

With a wide-screen HD monitor, it is thus possible to watch HD video on the PC. With a capacity of 25 GB, Blu-ray discs are ideal for large-scale backups. So what do you need to look for in a Blu-ray drive designed for PCs?

The first point to make regards the interface these drives use. Currently, they are available in USB, FireWire and SATA versions and, as with hard drives, all of these interfaces are more than capable of handling anything Blu-ray can throw at them. In other words, it doesn't matter which one you go for.

Then there is the issue of price. Drives that can write to a Blu-ray disc are twice as expensive as ones that just read a disc, so if you just want to watch Blu-ray video, buy a read-only model.

With regard to performance, top-end drives have read/write speeds of 10x/12x respectively, while low-end drives can manage only 4x/6x. Access times for top-end drives are around 150 ms, and 250 ms for low-end models.

If you want to use your Blu-ray drive to watch commercial movies on the PC, there are some other requirements apart from the drive itself.

First, the PC must be capable of handling the huge amounts of data that is involved with Blu-ray. This means a dual-core CPU is recommended, with a high-end Pentium or AMD equivalent, being the minimum. With regard to memory, 2 GB is recommended, with 1 GB being the minimum.

A further requirement is that both the video system (be it integrated video or a video card) and the monitor, must be HDCP (High-Bandwidth Digital Content Protection) compliant. If either is not, Blu-ray movies will not play on your PC.

While most recent video cards are HDCP complaint, there are many monitors on the market that are not, so this is an issue that needs to be checked in the specifications.

Hot tip

Blu-ray discs have a current maximum storage capacity of 25 GB. However, future projections are for discs with capacities of up to 200 GB.

Hot tip

High-bandwidth Digital Content Protection (HDCP) is a digital copy protection technology that prevents copying of digital audio and video content.

RDX Drives

RDX (Removable Disk Technology) is a disk-based storage technology that combines the best characteristics of tape drives and hard drives.

An RDX system comprises a docking bay, which can be mounted either externally or internally, and a removable cartridge that is inserted into a slot at the front of the docking bay. The cartridge itself is a standard 2.5 inch (laptop size) SATA 300 hard drive enclosed in a tough shock-resistant casing that is built to withstand physical abuse.

The RDX Quikstor from Tandberg

In operation, when a cartridge is inserted it is immediately detected by the operating system and assigned a drive letter. It can then be used in the same way as any other hard drive.

The advantages of RDX drives include:

- Portability – the cartridge can be quickly removed from the docking bay and slipped into a pocket (a large one)

- Reliability – the cartridge's casing is much tougher than that of an external hard drive or a tape cartridge

- Fast data transfer – as the cartridge is a hard drive, you get the speed and convenience of a hard drive

RDX drives are the ideal solution for those who need to transport large amounts of data easily and securely, and data backups. What really sets them apart from other types of portable drive is the ruggedness of the cartridges and their speed of operation.

Tape Drives

Tape drives are predominantly used in corporate environments and their purpose is to facilitate large-scale system backups. As such, they probably don't have too much relevance to the home PC builder. However, for anyone who may be interested in this type of drive, the following are available:

DAT (Digital Audio Tape) Drives

One of the oldest tape technologies, DAT was originally used for audio recording and uses 4mm tapes (similar in size to the old audio cassettes). These cartridges have a maximum capacity of 80 GB.

The latest version, DAT 320, has a maximum data transfer rate of 24 MBps, which will be seen on top-end models only. Low-end drives can be as slow as 7 MBps.

DLT (Digital Linear Tape) Drives

These devices use both side of the tape which, along with other innovations, vastly increases the amount of data a cartridge can hold (up to 800 GB).

Most DLT drives have a transfer rate of 20 MBps, but top-end models can transfer data at up to 32 MBps.

LTO (Linear Tape Open) Drives

LTO drives are currently the most popular type of tape drive, the reasons for which include: high-capacity cartridges, very fast data transfer rates, and drag & drop capability.

At the low-end, these drives can transfer data at 48 MBps, while at the high-end transfer rates can be as high as 240 MBps. Cartridge capacities range from 400 GB to 1600 GB (1.6 TB).

In general, tape drives are the most expensive type of removable media drive with LTO drives being the most expensive of all. However, once purchased this is mitigated to a certain degree by the relatively low cost of the cartridges. For example, 800 GB cartridges for LTO drives cost in the region of $50.

The big advantage of tape drives is the longevity of the cartridges with most types having a shelf life in the region of 35 years. Also, tape is the most reliable type of storage medium.

USB Flash Drives

A USB flash drive is a device that consists of a circuit board containing a NAND flash memory chip integrated with a USB interface.

These incredibly useful devices have seen off the ubiquitous floppy disk as they are smaller, faster, more robust, use very little power, and have much higher storage capacities.

Beware

Beware of fake USB drives being sold on eBay. Typically, these are the higher capacity models. The give-away is the ridiculously low price being charged. If you see one of these, it's not a bargain, it's a scam.

However, USB flash drives are not all made equal; some are decidedly better than others. While the most obvious difference is their capacity, this is not an indication of quality. To establish the quality of a drive, you need to consider the following factors:

The first is the type of flash memory used – SLC (single-level cell) or MLC (multi-level cell). Without going into the details, SLC is twice as fast as MLC. Furthermore, it lasts ten times as long. However, MLC memory is much cheaper, and so not surprisingly is the type used in most USB flash drives. SLC is only used in top-end drives.

Don't forget

Buyers may also care to look at the software offered with USB flash drives. Useful facilities offered with some are password protection and data encryption.

Unfortunately, the type of memory used is rarely, if ever, mentioned in the specifications. Therefore, buyers need to look at the data transfer rate specification. Low-end models (MLC) have a read speed of about 12 MBps and a write speed of about 5 MBps. High-end drives (SLC) have a read speed of 25 MBps and a write speed of 18 MBps – twice as fast.

Another important consideration with these drives is their build quality. Apart from being slow, cheap models are very flimsy affairs and, while they may work for a while, probably won't last too long. More expensive models on the other hand, are much more rugged in construction, and some of the top-end ones are built to withstand an enormous amount of physical abuse.

Installing a DVD Drive

Below, we see an ATA DVD drive being installed. The procedure for SATA drives is exactly the same as for SATA hard drives – see pages 123-124.

 Remove the front panel of the system case and then remove the appropriate blanking plate

2 Insert the drive from the front (if you try doing it from the back, the PSU may block access) and secure it in place

Hot tip

With modern DVD drives a separate audio cable is not necessary as they use the interface cable to make the connection to the sound system. These drives use a technology called Digital Audio Extraction (DAE).

3 If the drive has an audio cable (see top margin note) to connect it to the sound system, plug one end in the socket at the far left

Don't forget

80-pin interface cables are keyed to make sure they fit correctly. However, the older 40-pin cables are not, so it is possible to fit these the wrong way. If this is what you are using, keep the striped edge on the right.

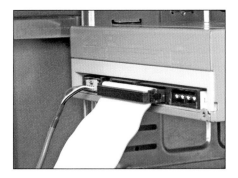

4 Keeping the striped edge to the right, plug the interface cable into the drive

...cont'd

You may need to consult the motherboard or sound card documentation to see where to connect the audio cable (assuming there is one).

5 Connect the Molex power supply connector

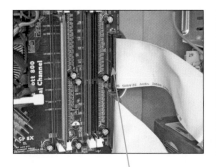

6 Connect the other end of the interface cable to the motherboard's socket

7 Connect the audio cable (if necessary) to the sound system

If you decide to install a second drive as well, the first step is to set it as the slave by changing the jumper settings as shown on the right.

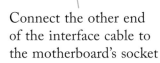

Then at step 4 (on the previous page), plug the slave connector (this will be in the middle of the interface cable and is usually a different color) into the drive. Otherwise, the procedure is exactly the same.

154

14 Setting Up the System

This chapter shows how to configure your new PC by setting up hardware devices, making changes in the BIOS, installing the operating system and installing system drivers.

Navigating the BIOS

The final stage of building your PC involves configuring some hardware devices in the BIOS and installing the operating system. To access the BIOS setup program, you need to press a key as the PC starts – see top margin note. When the BIOS opens, you'll see something similar to below depending on whether you have an AWARD or AMI BIOS.

```
              Phoenix - AwardBIOS CMOS Setup Utility

  ▶  Standard CMOS Features          ▶  Frequency/Uoltage Control

  ▶  Advanced BIOS Features             Load Fail-Safe Defaults

  ▶  Advanced Chipset Features          Load Optimized Defaults

  ▶  Integrated Peripherals             Set Supervisor Password

  ▶  Power Management Setup             Set User Password

  ▶  PnP/PCI Configurations             Save & Exit Setup

  ▶  PC Health Status                   Exit Without Saving


   Esc : Quit                     ↑ ↓ → ←     : Select Item
   F10 : Save & Exit Setup

              Time, Date, Hard Disk Type...
```

This is the main page and from it you can access pages specific to the various parts of the system. Note that your mouse will not work when navigating the BIOS; instead you have to use the following keys to scroll through the pages and change settings.

Key	Action
Up arrow	Moves the cursor up
Down arrow	Moves the cursor down
Left arrow	Moves the cursor left
Right arrow	Moves the cursor right
Page Up	Selects a higher value
Page Down	Selects a lower value
Enter	Makes a selection
Escape	Returns to the previous menu
F1	Opens the BIOS Help screen

Setting Up a Video Card

If you have installed a video card in your system, this is the first thing that needs to be set up by specifying what interface it uses in the BIOS.

If you are using a video system integrated in the motherboard, you can skip this step.

1. Enter the BIOS program and on the main BIOS page, select Advanced BIOS Features

2. Scroll to "Init Display First" and press Enter. A new menus will open from which you can select the relevant option (AGP, PCI, PCIE x16, etc). Press Enter again to confirm the selection and return to the previous screen

Don't forget

Unlike sound cards, a video card automatically disables integrated video when it is installed.

```
          Phoenix - AwardBIOS CMOS Setup Utility
                  Advanced BIOS Features

 Hard Disk Boot Priority    [Press Enter]         Item Help
 First Boot Device          [Floppy]
 Second Boot Device         [Hard Drive]       Menu Level    ▶
 Third Boot Device          [CD-ROM]
 Boot Up Floppy Seek        [Disabled]
 Boot Up Num-Lock           [On]
 Password Check             [Setup]
 Interrupt Mode             [APIC]
 HDD S.M.A.R.T. Capability  [Disabled]
 Init Display First         [ PCIEx16 ]




 ↑↓→←:Move  Enter:Select  +/-/PU/PD:Value  F10:Save  Esc:Exit F1:Help
   F5: Previous Values  F6: Fail-Safe Defaults  F7: Optimized Defaults
```

Note that motherboards usually denote the PCI-Express x16 option as PCIE x16. In some boards it may be denoted as PEG.

Also, if your motherboard has two or more PCI-Express x16 slots, you will have options for PCIE x16-1, PCIE x16-2, PCIE x16-3, etc. The figure at the end identifies the slot and the 1 socket will be the topmost on the board, the 2 slot the next one down, and so on. Make sure you select the socket the card is installed in.

Enabling USB

Next, enable USB. For some reason, many BIOSs come with it disabled.

1 On the main BIOS page, select Integrated Peripherals and press Enter

```
                Phoenix - AwardBIOS CMOS Setup Utility

   ▶ Standard CMOS Features          ▶ Frequency/Uoltage Control

   ▶ Advanced BIOS Features            Load Fail-Safe Defaults

   ▶ Advanced Chipset Features         Load Optimized Defaults

   ▶ Integrated Peripherals            Set Supervisor Password

   ▶ Power Management Setup            Set User Password

   ▶ PnP/PCI Configurations           Save & Exit Setup

   ▶ PC Health Status                 Exit Without Saving


    Esc : Quit                     ↑ ↓ → ←    : Select Item
    F10 : Save & Exit Setup

              Onboard IO, IRQ, DMA Assignment ...
```

Hot tip

While you have the Integrated Peripherals screen open, scroll down and check to see if your board provides USB 3. If it does, you will see a Onboard USB 3.0 Controller option. Make sure this is enabled as well.

2 Scroll to USB Controllers and press Enter to open the Options screen

```
                Phoenix - AwardBIOS CMOS Setup Utility
                      Integrated Peripherals

   ICH SATA Control Mode       [AHCI]           Item Help
   SATA Port0-3 Native Mode    [Enabled]
 ▶ USB Controllers            [Press Enter]
   USB Keyboard Function       [Enabled]       Menu Level  ▶
   USB Mouse Function          [Enabled]
   USB Storage Function        [Enabled]
   Azalia Codec                [Disabled]
   Onboard H/W 1394            [Enabled]
   Onboard H/W LAN             [Enabled]
   Green LAN                   [Disabled
 ▶ Smart LAN                  [Press Enter]
   Onboard LAN Boot ROM        [Disabled]
   Onboard USB 3.0 Controller  [Enabled]
   eSATA Controller            [Enabled]
   eSATA Ctrl Mode             [IDE]
   GSATA 6-7/IDE Controller    [Enabled]
   GSATA 6-7/IDE Ctrl Mode     [IDE]
   SATA3 Firmware Selection    [Auto]
```

3 Select Enabled and then press Enter to confirm the selection and return to the main screen

Disabling Integrated Sound

All motherboards come with the integrated sound system enabled by default in the BIOS. If you intend to use a sound card, you must disable it.

If you are planning to use a sound card in your computer, it will be necessary to disable the motherboard's integrated sound system.

1 Open the Integrated Peripherals page and locate the entry that relates to the motherboard's integrated sound. In the screenshot below, it is the Azalia codec but this will probably be different in your board. If in doubt, the motherboard's manual will specify what to look for

2 Scroll to the appropriate setting, which will currently be Enabled, and press Enter to open the Options screen. Select Disabled and press Enter again.

```
            Phoenix - AwardBIOS CMOS Setup Utility
                    Integrated Peripherals

   ICH SATA Control Mode       [AHCI]                  Item Help
   SATA Port0-3 Native Mode    [Enabled]
 ▶ USB Controllers             [Press Enter]
   USB Keyboard Function       [Enabled]            Menu Level    ▶
   USB Mouse Function          [Enabled]
   USB Storage Function        [Enabled]
   Azalia Codec                [Disabled]
   Onboard H/W 1394            [Enabled]
   Onboard H/W LAN             [Enabled]
   Green LAN                   [Disabled]
 ▶ Smart LAN                   [Press Enter]
   Onboard LAN Boot ROM        [Disabled]
   Onboard USB 3.0 Controller  [Enabled]
   eSATA Controller            [Enabled]
   eSATA Ctrl Mode             [IDE]
   GSATA 6-7/IDE Controller    [Enabled]
   GSATA 6-7/IDE Ctrl Mode     [IDE]
   SATA3 Firmware Selection    [Auto]
```

When you run Windows for the first time, you will then have to install the sound card's driver.

Setting the Boot Device

The next thing that needs to be done is to configure the hard drive to your requirements, and then install the operating system (we are going to use Windows 7 in this chapter).

Because Windows comes on a DVD, we have to set the BIOS to boot from the CD/DVD drive (by default, it is set to boot from the Floppy Drive).

This is done as follows:

 On the main BIOS page, scroll to Advanced BIOS Features and press Enter

 On the next page, scroll down to First Boot Device. Using the Page Up/Page Down keys, cycle through the options and select the CDROM option

```
            Phoenix - AwardBIOS CMOS Setup Utility
                    Advanced BIOS Features

    Virus Warning             [Disabled]        Item Help
    CPU Internal Cache        [Enabled]
    External Cache            [Enabled]      Menu Level  ►
    CPU L2 Cache ECC Checking  [Enabled]
    Quick Power On Self Test  [Enabled]      Select Your Boot
    First Boot Device         [CDROM]        Device Priority.
    Second Boot Device        [HDD-O]
    Third Boot Device         [CDROM]
    Boot Other Device         [Enabled]
    Swap Floppy Drive         [Disabled]
    Boot Up Floppy Seek       [Enabled]
    Bootup NumLock Status     [On]
    Gate A20 Option           [Fast]
    Typematic Rate Setting    [Disabled]
  X Typematic Rate (Chars/Sec) 6
  X Typematic Delay (Msec)     250
    Security Option           [Setup]
    OS Select For Dram > 64MB  [Non-OS2]
    HDD S.M.A.R.T Capability  [Enabled]
```

3 Press the Escape key to return to the main page

Unless you intend to set up your hard drives in a RAID configuration (see pages 161-162), your BIOS changes are now complete. Note that you must save the changes before exiting the BIOS program, otherwise they will revert to the original settings. The option for this is on the main BIOS page at the right-hand side (Save & Exit Setup).

Don't forget

Before you exit the BIOS, save your changes. A quick way is to press the F10 key. This works with both AWARD and AMI BIOSs.

RAID Configurations

The next stage is to install Windows. Before you do though, you may wish to take advantage of a hard drive setup known as RAID (Redundant Array of Independent Disks).

RAID is a way of configuring a combination of hard drives to gain specific benefits, and it requires at least two drives.

Of the various RAID configurations, the ones described below may be of interest in a home-PC environment.

RAID 0
This requires a minimum of two drives, (preferably identical) and works by splitting (known as striping) the data equally between them. The result is much improved data transfer speeds (up to 50 per cent) as each drive handles part of a file.

RAID 1
This also requires a minimum of two drives. In this configuration, all data saved is duplicated (known as mirroring) on each drive. The purpose is data protection – if one drive fails, the data is recoverable from the other/s.

RAID 0/1
This is a combination of RAID 0 and RAID 1 and requires a minimum of four drives. Half the drives are used to stripe the data, and the other half to mirror it. Thus, it provides fast data transfer, together with data protection.

RAID 5
This requires a minimum of three drives. Data is striped across all the drives but an error checking bit (known as the parity bit) is also stored. Should any one drive fail, the RAID controller will calculate the missing data (using the parity bit) and keep the system running until the faulty drive can be replaced.

To implement RAID, you need a RAID controller, which sets up and maintains the configuration. This will be provided by the motherboard in the form of a integrated controller.

Alternatively, you can install a hardware based RAID controller card (shown right) if you want a higher quality RAID setup. The software based controllers provided by motherboards are perfectly adequate for home PC use, however. The next page shows how it's done.

Hot tip

Note that with RAID 0, the capacity of the setup will be the sum of the drives, e.g. two 320 GB drives will be seen by Windows as a single drive with a capacity of 640 GB.

With RAID 1, the capacity of one of the drives is lost so using the example above, Windows will see one drive with a capacity of 320 GB.

...cont'd

The method of creating a RAID array depends on your hardware. High-end motherboards usually provide a Windows RAID utility that allows the user to install the operating system on a single drive and then create and modify the RAID array from Windows.

Most motherboards however, do not provide this facility in which case it has to be done in the BIOS. The instructions for how to access the BIOS RAID utility will be in the motherboard manual. When you open the utility, you will see something similar to the screenshot below:

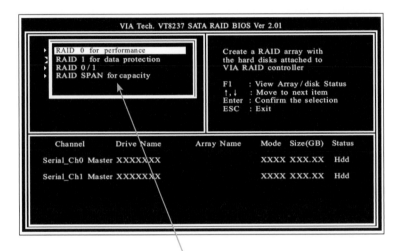

Typically, you will be given four options: RAID 0, RAID 1, RAID 0/1 and RAID Span. Make your choice and press Enter.

To make the task easier, most BIOS RAID setup utilities offer an auto-setup option. All you have to do is specify the configuration required which, in the example above, is RAID 0. The utility will then set up the configuration automatically; the process taking only a few seconds. Reboot and you're done.

A two-drive RAID 0 setup provides a huge boost in drive speed and is an ideal way of turning two low-end, and thus cheap, drives into one high performance unit. The downside, of course, is that there is a 50 per cent greater chance of losing your data as a result of drive failure. Also, it is not unknown for software based motherboard RAID controllers to malfunction with the same result. This is why a dedicated hardware RAID controller card, which provides a more reliable setup, should be used when your data is mission-critical.

Hot tip

Software RAID controllers as provided by motherboards are not as reliable as hardware RAID controller cards. They also offer lower performance levels.

Hot tip

A two-drive RAID 0 setup should provide a performance increase of around 50 per cent. Adding a third drive should increase it by a further 30 per cent, and a fourth drive by about 20 per cent, and so on.

Hot tip

The danger of a RAID 0 setup is that you have a much greater chance of losing your data due to hard drive failure.

Installing Windows

The first thing here is to get the hard drive operational by partitioning and then formatting it. With both Windows Vista and Windows 7, these processes are part of the respective operating system's installation procedure.

Proceed as follows:

 1 Configure the system to boot from the CD/DVD drive as described on page 160

2 Place the Windows installation disk in the CD/DVD drive and then boot the PC

3 When you see a message saying "press any key to boot from CD...", do so

Windows will now load its installation files from the disk. You will then see the following screen:

4 Select the required language, and time and currency format, and then click Next. In the screen that opens, click the "Install Now" button.

Don't forget

Before any internal hard disk drive can be used, it has to be partitioned and formatted. If you don't do it, while the drive will be recognized by the BIOS, it won't be by the operating system.

Hot tip

Partitioning is the process of defining specific areas of the hard disk for the operating system to use.

  Formatting prepares a disk to receive data by organizing it into logical units called blocks, sectors and tracks. These enable the drive's read/write heads to accurately position and locate data.

...cont'd

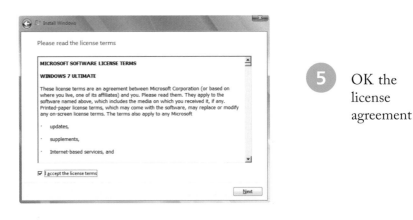

5 OK the license agreement

When installing any operating system, it is always advisable to do a clean installation (the Custom [advanced] option in step 6).

6 For the type of installation, select the Custom (advanced) option

7 In the "Where do you want to install Windows?" screen, you'll see your unformatted and unpartitioned hard drive. Click Drive options (advanced)

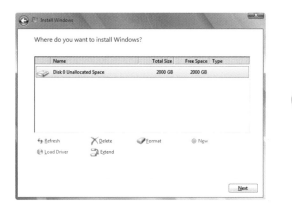

8 Click New

If you are installing Windows Vista, at step 9 you will also have to click the Format button. With Windows 7, this is done automatically.

9 Click Apply to create a single partition equal to the size of the drive

Hot tip

At step 9, Windows automatically creates a partition equal to the total capacity of the drive. However, you have the option of creating two or more partitions by entering a lower number in the "Size" box and then clicking New.

Click Next, and the Windows installation procedure will begin. It should take between 10 and 30 minutes to complete depending on the speed of your PC.

Installing System Drivers

When you run Windows for the first time, the first thing to do is complete the setting up by installing essential system drivers. The most important of these are the motherboard drivers.

All you have to do is place the motherboard's installation disk in the CD/DVD drive and Windows AutoPlay will automatically open the disk's Setup utility.

Typically, this will give you an easy option, whereby the drivers will be installed along with various other utilities that you may or not want; and an Advanced option, which allows you to choose what is installed.

To complete the installation of the motherboard's drivers, you will be asked to reboot the PC. When back in Windows, the next step is to install the drivers for any hardware connected to the computer. Typically, these include Video cards, Sound cards, Printers, Routers, Monitors, Mice and keyboards.

Finally, install your programs. While your system is new and performing at its best, we recommend that you benchmark it (see bottom margin note). This will enable you to monitor the system over time, and thus identify any issues that may be causing performance degradation.

15 Peripherals

In this chapter, we take a look at the more common types of peripheral, such as scanners and printers and explain what you need to look for to ensure you get a good quality device. We also look at broadband modems, devices essential for an Internet connection.

Printers

Printers suitable for PC users come in two basic types: ink-jets and lasers. Both have pros and cons that make them suitable for some purposes and less so for others.

Standard Ink-Jet Printers

These printers can be considered to be all-rounders as they produce good results with both text and images. This, together with their low price, makes them the ideal printer for home users.

They do have some drawbacks, however:

- Print quality for both text and images, while perfectly adequate for most purposes, is not the best

- Print speeds are slow; this makes them unsuitable for large-scale print jobs

- The ink cartridges are extremely expensive, which makes these printers suitable for occasional use only

When buying an ink-jet, consider the following:

Print Resolution (dpi)

Letter quality requires a resolution of 600 dpi, while images need one of 1200. All current ink-jets are capable of both but be aware that high-quality photograph printing will require a resolution of 2400 dpi or higher.

Paper Handling

Mainstream ink-jets will print letter size or smaller. If you need to print larger documents, you will need to buy a business class model, which will be considerably more expensive. If you envisage having long print jobs, check out the capacity of the paper input tray. Low-end models will hold no more than 50 sheets or so; high-end models will hold about 150.

Print Speed

This is quoted as pages per minute (PPM), for both color and black and white. Use this specification for comparison purposes only though, as it rarely reflects real world performance.

Build Quality

Printers at the low-end of the market tend to be flimsy affairs. If you buy one of these, expect to be replacing it before too long.

Photo Printers

With the increasing use of PCs for storing and editing images, photo printers have become extremely popular. They also use ink-jet technology but take it to a different level in terms of print quality.

They achieve this by using much higher print resolutions and by using a wider range of colored inks than standard ink-jets do. As a result, print quality approaches that of professional print labs.

Photo printers are also quicker than standard ink-jets, which can take an eternity to print a photo at a high setting. Another feature they offer is the ability to read directly from flash memory cards, such as those used by digital cameras. Many also offer an LCD to view your photos, not to mention editing facilities such as crop, rotate, brightness and contrast adjustment, etc.

Things to look out for when buying a photo printer include:

Ink Cartridges

Photo printers, typically, use between four and six different inks, and generally, the ones that use six will produce higher quality prints than those which use less.

You should also be aware that some use a single cartridge that contains all the inks, so if one color runs out, the cartridge has to be replaced even though the other colors haven't. Therefore, running costs can be cut substantially by choosing a model in which each color is held in a separate cartridge.

Memory Card Reader

If you want to take advantage of the direct printing facility offered by these printers, make sure it can read the type of memory card that you use. In particular, look for PictBridge support.

Print Size

Some photo printers have a maximum print size of 4 x 6 inches. If you want larger sizes, be sure to check the specifications.

Beware

Note that many photo printers are not so good at printing text, as they are designed for smooth color blending rather than sharp lines. That said, if your requirements aren't too high in this respect, most of them are quite adequate.

Hot tip

PictBridge is a standardized technology that lets you transfer images from the memory card in a digital camera directly to a printer. Print size, layout, date, and other settings can be set within the camera. However, both the printer and the camera must support PictBridge.

...cont'd

Laser Printers

Laser technology is completely different from ink-jet and produces much better results in terms of print speed and quality. Laser printers also offer much more in the way of features, such as high-capacity paper trays and duplexing (a facility that allows printing on both sides of the paper).

They also have much lower running costs than ink-jets.

The main drawback is the higher initial cost, although it must be said that low-end lasers are now not much more expensive than ink-jets.

Another drawback is the fact that low-end models are not as good at printing high-quality photographs as photo ink-jets are (you will need at least a mid-range laser for this).

However, if you do serious amounts of printing, or require very high text quality then a laser printer has to be the choice.

If you decide to buy one of these devices, apart from the considerations already mentioned on page 168, you should look at the following:

Toner and Drum

These are the two main consumables in a laser printer. With some lasers, the toner (laser equivalent of ink) and drum are combined in a replaceable cartridge, while with others they are separate parts. The problem with the cartridge type is that the toner will run out long before the drum needs to be replaced. While some cartridges can be refilled with toner, others can't, so to keep running costs down avoid the latter.

Memory

Laser printers come with built-in memory but low-end models are often supplied with a minimal amount of it – usually just enough to allow low-resolution printing. So check that you can upgrade the memory should it be necessary to do so.

170

Hot tip

A useful advantage color lasers have over ink-jets is that they do not need expensive glossy paper to print high-quality photos. Prints look just as good on matt paper.

Installing a Printer

Printers are simple devices to install – as long as you follow the manufacturer's instructions. Typically, they will be as follows:

 Install the printer's driver from the installation disk

 Connect the printer's USB cable to the computer

Don't forget

Make sure that you read the printer's installation instructions. While the procedure described on the left is typical for most current printers, it's not set in stone.

 Switch the printer on

Windows will then recognize and configure the device, after which it will be ready for use. If you don't follow the above sequence, you may well experience problems.

Multi-Function Devices

Multi-function units consist of a printer and a scanner, which also combine to act as a copier and sometimes a fax machine, all incorporated within the same housing.

The advantages they offer are convenience (one connection to the PC, one wall socket required), less desktop space than would be required by stand-alone devices and a cost saving compared to buying the devices separately. These make them a very attractive option to many users.

The big disadvantage (potentially) is that if something goes wrong with the machine, the user may well lose all of its functions. In a business environment this could well be seriously inconvenient.

As regards buying one, you should look at the specifications of each incorporated device just as you would when buying stand-alone devices.

Beware

A potential problem with multi-function devices is that if they go wrong, the user may lose all the functions that they provide.

Broadband Modems

Broadband Modems

If broadband is available in your area, you ought to seriously consider signing up for it. It has many advantages and will revolutionize the way you use the Internet.

Broadband comes in several versions, each of which require the use of a specialized modem.

- DSL and ADSL – works on telephone lines with speeds up to 50 Mbps (although few ISPs offer anything higher than 20 Mbps)

- Cable – works on CATV cable networks and provides similar speeds to DSL and ADSL

- Satellite – for people living in remote locations, a satellite connection is an option. It is available with speeds of up to 20 Mbps. It is expensive though and is also the least reliable as it can be adversely affected by weather conditions

Of the three types, cable is the one recommended as it is the easiest to set up and also the most reliable. However, not everyone has access to a cable network and if this is the case, DSL is the next best option.

The modem will connect to the computer via either USB or Ethernet. For simplicity of installation, USB is the easiest. An Ethernet connection will also require an Ethernet PCI card to be installed in the PC, unless the motherboard has an integrated Ethernet interface – most do these days.

Virtually all ISPs will supply a modem as part of the package (and charge you rental accordingly), so this is not something you need to consider unless of course you buy your own modem, which may allow you to negotiate a lower price with the ISP.

With regard to specifications, this is not something you need to investigate.

A feature available with some modems that's worth having, is a built-in hardware firewall. Firewalls are essential for broadband connections and most people use a software version, which tend not to be as good as the hardware type.

Hot tip

Broadband speed is measured in Megabits per second (Mbps). Don't confuse this with Megabytes per second (MBps), which is the metric used for file sizes, download limits, etc.

8 Megabits is equivalent to 1Megabyte.

Hot tip

If you are fortunate enough to have a choice, cable broadband is the recommended option. It's quick, reliable and easy to set up.

Installing a Broadband Modem

Usually, this will be done by the ISP. However, should you have to do it yourself for some reason, the procedure is as follows:

The first step is to extend the signal input from its entry point to the house, to where the modem is located. For this you will need a suitable length of coaxial cable and the appropriate connectors.

If you are tapping into your TV's cable input, you will also need a signal splitter, as shown above. Connect the signal cable to the splitter's input, connect the TV to one output and the modem's cable to the other output. Then run the latter to the modem.

Don't forget

If you are connecting an Ethernet modem to a Ethernet adapter built-in to the motherboard, remember that it will be necessary to install the Ethernet driver from the motherboard's installation disk.

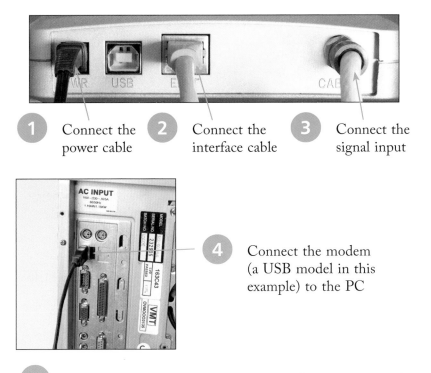

1 Connect the power cable

2 Connect the interface cable

3 Connect the signal input

4 Connect the modem (a USB model in this example) to the PC

Don't forget

When running the modem for the first time, be aware that it may need several minutes to synchronize itself with the network. During this period, you will be unable to access the Internet.

5 Switch the PC on. If you are running Windows 7, which has virtually all current modem drivers built-in, you won't have to bother with installation disks as setup will be done automatically. Otherwise, a disk may be necessary.

Scanners

Scanners are devices that are by no means essential, but can turn out to be surprisingly useful in many ways. For home-users, the flatbed type (shown right) is the best one to go for.

When deciding which scanner to buy, you need to consider the following specifications:

Resolution
This is a measure of the detail reproduced by the scan process and is expressed in dots per inch (dpi). The table below shows the resolution required by the most common applications.

Application	Resolution
Images for commercial printing	300 dpi
Images to be enlarged	300 dpi upwards
Negatives and Slides	1200 dpi minimum
Images for printing on ink-jet printers	200 to 300 dpi
Text documents	300 dpi
Line art (drawings, diagrams, etc)	300 dpi
Images for websites, viewing on monitors	72 dpi

Optical Density
Also known as Dynamic Range, this indicates how wide a range of tones the scanner can recognize and is measured on a scale from 0.0 (perfect white) to 4.0 (perfect black).

Most flatbed scanners have an OD around 2.8 to 3.0, which is fine for photographs. Slides, negatives and transparencies, which have broader tonal ranges, will need a higher OD of about 3.4.

Interface
Virtually all scanners intended for home use use the USB interface. For typical applications, this is all you need. SCSI models are available but are considerably more expensive.

Accessories
Some scanners include useful accessories such as slide and negative attachments and sheet feeders.

Speakers

A good set of speakers is an integral part of a high-quality sound system. You may have the best sound card in the galaxy but if it is connected to a cheap speaker system, you will get poor sound.

PC speakers are available either as a pair or as a multiple speaker system. The type of setup you go for depends on the intended use.

Music buffs who simply want high-fidelity will be best served by a pair of high-quality stereo speakers – a surround-sound system is not necessary.

Gamers and DVD movie fans who do want surround-sound will need a multiple speaker system, as shown below. When buying one of these, don't forget to check that your sound system is capable of fully utilizing it. There's no point in buying a 9.1 speaker system if you have only three line-out jacks, for example.

Whichever type of setup you go for, considering the following specifications will ensure that your chosen speakers are up to scratch.

Frequency Response
This is the range of frequencies that the speakers can reproduce. The closer it is to the 20 Hz (bass) and 20 KHz (treble) thresholds, the better the output quality.

Sensitivity
This is sometimes referred to as Sound Pressure Level in specification sheets and indicates the efficiency with which the speakers convert power to sound. Look for a figure of at least 90 decibels.

Wattage Rating
While this is not a true indication of quality, it is a fact that speakers with a high wattage rating do generally produce better sound.

Hot tip

The wider a speaker's frequency range, the better its quality. Low-frequency response is essential for good bass reproduction, while high-frequency response is essential for good treble reproduction.

Hot tip

Speaker wattage is rated in two ways: peak power and continuous (RMS) power. The manufacturers like to emphasize the former as this is the higher of the two figures. However, buyers should be more concerned with the continuous power rating as this gives a more accurate indication of the speaker's capabilities.

Speaker Installation

This is a simple enough exercise. However, it is remarkable how many people get it wrong, connecting the speakers to either the wrong sound system (integrated instead of the sound card or vice versa) or to the wrong jack.

The input/output ports of a basic sound card are shown below:

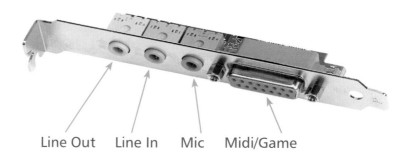

Line Out   Line In   Mic   Midi/Game

The speakers connect to the green line out jack. Use any other jack and you will not get any sound from the PC. With the card shown above you will only be able to use a two-speaker setup as it only has one line out jack.

Advanced sound cards offer more in the way of connectivity as demonstrated by the input/output panel of the card shown below:

Here, the green, black and two orange jacks all provide a line out connection. The pink jack is for a microphone, the blue jack is for line in, and finally, there are input and output sockets for S/PDIF coaxial cables – see margin note.

In multiple-speaker setups, the green line out jack is used for the front speakers, the black jack for the rear speakers and the orange jacks for the center and side speakers.

As it has four line out jacks, the card shown above can support eight speakers.

Hot tip

Most sound cards provide color-coded input and output jacks for easy identification.

Green – line out
Orange – line out
Black – line out
Blue – line in
Pink – microphone

Hot tip

S/PDIF stands for Sony/Philips Digital Interface; a standard audio file transfer format. Developed jointly by the Sony and Phillips corporations, S/PDIF allows the transfer of digital audio signals from one device to another without having to be first converted to an analog format, which has a degrading effect on the quality of the signal.

16 Troubleshooting

If all goes to plan, you won't need to read this chapter. However, if you do encounter a problem or two along the way, it may help to resolve the issue.

Hard Drives

Hard Drive Failure

When you start the computer, on the first boot screen you should see the hard drive listed (the Samsung HD103SJ in the example below). If it is, this indicates that the BIOS has recognized the drive and configured it correctly.

Don't forget

Note that the screenshots and procedures described in this chapter relate to a system running Windows 7. Those of you running Windows Vista will find they are very similar, however.

```
    Award Modular BIOS v6.00PC
    Copyright (C) 1984-2010, Award Software, Inc

    X58A-UD3R FB

    Main Processor : Intel (R) Core(TM) i7 CPU 3.74GHz (178x22)
    <CPUID :000106A5 Patch ID :00000011>
    Memory Testing : 6290432K OK

    Memory Frequency 1360MHz
    Detecting IDE Drives ...
    IDE Channel 0 Master : Samsung HD103SJ 1AJ10001
    IDE Channel 1 Master : ASUS DRW-2014L1




    <Del> :BIOS Setup <F9> :XpressRecovery2 <F12> :Boot Menu <End> Qflasl
    08/24/2010-X58-ICH10-7A89QGONC-00
```

If it isn't there, the BIOS isn't "seeing" it. Depending on the BIOS in your system, one of two things will happen.

1) Boot-up will stop at this point

2) Boot-up will continue and then stop with a "Disk Boot Failure" error message

Hot tip

If the system doesn't recognize the hard drive and assuming the device is not faulty, the problem is most likely to be a loose or incorrect connection.

```
                                              L2 Cache Size    :    64K

    Diskette Drive A  : 1.44M 3.5 in         Display Type     : EGA/VGA
    Diskette Drive B  : None                 Serial Ports     : 3FB
    Pri. Master Disk  : None                 Parallel Port(s) : 378
    Pri. Slave Disk   : None                 DDR SDRAM at Bank : 1
    Sec. Master Disk  : None
    Sec. Slave Disk   : CD-RW, ATA 33


    PCI Device Listing
    Bus No. Device No. Func No. Vendor/Device Class Device Class               IRQ
        0      16        0      1106   3038  0C03  USB 1.0/1.1 UHCI Cntrlr      11
        0      16        1      1106   3038  0C03  USB 1.0/1.1 UHCI Cntrlr      11
        0      16        2      1106   3038  0C03  USB 1.0/1.1 UHCI Cntrlr       5
        0      16        3      1106   3104  0C03  USB 2.0 UHCI Cntrlr           3
        0      17        1      1106   0571  0101  IDE Cntrlr                   14
        0      17        5      1106   3059  0401  Multimedia Device             5
        1       0        0      1002   5961  0300  Display Cntrlr               11
                                                   ACPI Controller               9

    Verifying DMI Pool Data
    Boot From CD :
    DISK BOOT FAILURE, INSERT SYSTEM DISK AND PRESS ENTER
    -
```

There are four possible causes of this:

1) The drive is not powered up
2) The drive is not connected correctly
3) The drive is faulty
4) The system is configured to boot from a non-boot drive

The latter is the first thing to check and if you have two or more hard drives in the system, is quite likely to be the cause of the problem. Go into the BIOS, open the Advanced Features page, select "Hard drive priority" and make sure the boot drive (the one Windows is installed on) is specified as the first drive.

The next thing to check is that the drive is getting power from the power supply unit. The easiest way to do this is to connect a different power connector that you know is working; for example, the one powering the CD/DVD drive. Also, check that the drive is properly connected to the motherboard. Remake the interface connections and check that they are correct.

If the drive is getting power and the connections are OK, then the device is faulty. This is very unlikely though and invariably the fault will be a connection issue.

Another problem that can occur is the boot procedure stopping at the "Verifying DMI Pool Data" stage. DMI pool data is hardware related information that is passed from the BIOS to the operating system during bootup, and if the BIOS finds an error during the verification stage, the boot procedure may stop at this point.

The usual cause is a connection issue but it can also be the result of a transient configuration problem that can be resolved by simply switching off and then back on again. This is the first thing to try. If the problem persists, however, you almost certainly have a bad connection somewhere.

Check the drive's connections and try again. If the boot procedure still hangs, disconnect all non-boot drives, i.e. DVD drives, external hard drives, flash drives, as it's possible the system is trying to boot from one of them rather than the boot drive.

If there is still no joy, reseat all expansion boards connected to the PC, e.g. sound and video cards, TV tuner cards, etc.

The last resort is to replace the drive.

Don't forget

If you install two or more hard drives in your system, remember to check that the boot drive has priority in the BIOS. This is the drive in which the BIOS will expect to find the operating system.

179

Video

An important thing to be aware of with regard to video, is that if anything is visible on the screen, even a single dot, it is working (to a certain degree at any rate).

A common scenario is the boot procedure reaching the stage where Windows begins to load and then stopping with a blank screen. While this can be a problem with Windows itself, another possible cause is the video system and, usually, is a result of the video system driver having become corrupted.

The solution is to boot into Windows using the Safe Mode option, and you do it by rebooting and then tapping the F8 key repeatedly until the Windows Advanced Options menus appears as shown below:

```
Windows Advanced Options Menu
Please select An Option

Safe Mode
Safe Mode With Networking
Safe Mode With Command Prompt

Enable Boot Logging
Enable VGA Mode
Last Known Good Configuration (Yout Most Recent Settings That Worked)
Directory Services Restore Mode (Windows Domain Controllers Only)

Start Windows Normally
Reboot
Return To OS Choices Menu

Use the up and down arrow keys to move the highlight to your choice
```

Using the arrow keys, select Safe Mode and then reboot. This should get you back into Windows and allow you to reinstall the video driver.

If you are using a PCI-Express video card and have no video at all, check that the card's 4-pin power supply is properly connected. While this is unlikely to have come adrift if it was connected properly in the first place, if it wasn't it may eventually work loose with a resulting lack of video.

If your video has been working but suddenly slows down to the point where you can literally see it being drawn on the screen, the cause, again, is a corrupted or missing video driver. Simply reinstall it and all should be well.

Windows

If you find yourself in a situation where all your hardware checks out but you cannot boot into Windows, then the most obvious culprit is Windows itself.

The most usual cause of Windows refusing to start is corrupted startup files and, fortunately, this is an easy issue to remedy. Do it as follows:

Hot tip

If Startup Repair fails to get Windows running, you have a hardware problem. Disconnect all non-essential hardware, i.e. strip the system down to the bare minimum necessary for the computer to run. Then try again. If Windows now loads, reinstall your hardware devices one-by-one, rebooting each time, until you have identified the problem device.

1. Go into the BIOS and set the CD/DVD drive as the first boot device – see page 160

2. Reboot the PC with the Windows installation disk in the CD/DVD drive. When you see a message saying "Press any key to boot from the CD drive ...", do so

3. The Windows Boot Manager will open. Select the Windows Setup [EMS enabled] option and click Next. This opens the Windows installation screen

4. Click Next and then click Repair your computer. In the screen that opens, click Next

5. Now you will see the System Recovery Options screen as shown below. Select the first option, Startup Repair and click Next

Windows will now repair the system's startup files. When you are prompted to restart, do so. The PC should now boot into Windows.

Sound

If the computer isn't communicating with you audibly, the first and most obvious thing to check is the system's volume level. Click the loudspeaker icon at the right-hand side of the Taskbar and make sure the slider hasn't been dragged to the off position. Also check that the speakers haven't been muted.

The next step is to check that the sound system is correctly installed.

1   Go to Start, Control Panel and click Sounds.

2   Under the Playback and Recording tabs, check that your sound device is listed. If it is, the driver is OK – go to paragraph seven on the next page

3   If the sound device isn't listed, it needs to be installed using the installation disk

182

In the unlikely event that you still have no sound after this, try checking for problems in the Device Manager.

Go to Start, Control Panel, Device Manager. Expand the Sound, Video and Game Controllers category, locate the sound system and see if there's a warning symbol next to it.

If there is, right-click the device, click Properties, and the nature of the problem will be revealed in the next dialog box.

If you are using a sound card and Device Manager reports no problems, check the card is firmly seated in its socket on the motherboard.

Then check that you have disabled the motherboard's integrated sound system – see page 159. Also, check the speakers are actually connected to the card and not to the integrated sound system.

Finally, try a different card.

If the Sounds dialog box indicates that the sound device is correctly installed (page 182, Step 2), then check the speakers are connected to the correct jack, i.e. 'Speaker Out', 'Audio Out' or 'Line Out'.

Finally, if you are using speakers that need their own power supply, make sure they are getting it and that the speaker volume control is turned up.

Hot tip

The Device Manager is the place to go when you are having problems with your hardware. Very often, the nature of a fault will be detailed here together with a solution.

Don't forget

If you are using a sound card, make sure the speakers are connected to the sound card and not the motherboard's sound system.

Removable Media Drives

Usually, when these devices have a physical problem, the relevant drive icon will be missing in My Computer.

Boot the PC and on the first boot screen you should see the drive listed. If it isn't, the drive is either faulty or it has a connection problem. Open the system case and check that the power and interface cables are securely connected. If the BIOS still doesn't recognize the drive, it is faulty.

If the drive is listed on the boot screen but not in My Computer then it has a configuration problem (see margin note). See if the drive is listed in Device Manager under the DVD/CD-ROM category and whether any problems are reported there. If so, try the suggested remedy. Failing that, do the following:

1   In the Device Manager, right-click the device and click Uninstall

![Device Manager screenshot showing DVD/CD-ROM drives context menu with Uninstall option]

2   Switch the PC off and physically disconnect the drive by removing both the power and interface cables. Then reconnect them and reboot. Windows will see the device as a new addition to the system and automatically assign it a new channel, which should resolve the issue

If the drive isn't listed in Device Manager, follow the procedure described in Step 2 above.

Printers

Printers are probably the most likely of all the devices in a computer system to cause trouble. However, in most cases the problem will not be the printer itself, but rather its installation in Windows. It could also be the connection to the PC.

Printer Test Page
The first thing to do is eliminate the printer as the cause of the issue and this is done with the Printer Test Page check.

Refer to the manual for instructions on how to do this as the procedure varies from printer to printer. Usually, it is done by disconnecting the device's interface cable from the computer and then pressing a combination of buttons on the printer. If the test is successful, it establishes that the printer itself is OK and that the fault is either software-related or with the connections.

Printer Connections
Assuming the test page does print as it should, then the next thing to check is that the printer cables are OK and connected to the correct ports. It is unlikely that there will be anything wrong with the printer interface cable itself, but do check that the connections to both the printer and the PC are sound.

Is The Printer Installed?
Go to Start, Control Panel and click Devices and Printers.

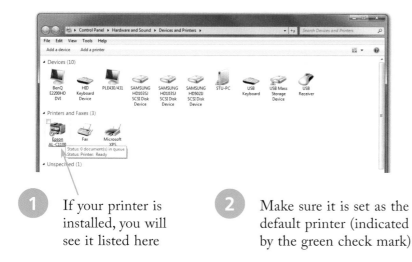

1 If your printer is installed, you will see it listed here

2 Make sure it is set as the default printer (indicated by the green check mark)

If the printer isn't listed, it hasn't been installed, or has been installed incorrectly. Reinstall it as described on page 171.

Don't forget

All printers have the facility to print a test page, For instructions on how to do it on your model, refer to the printer's documentation.

Broadband

If you cannot access the Internet via your broadband connection, the first thing to check is that the modem is communicating with the computer. You can do this by taking a look at the modem's front panel. Here, you will see a row of LEDs. Two of these, USB and ENET (Ethernet), indicate whether the respective connection is working.

In the example below, we can see that the modem is connected to the PC via USB and that the connection is OK.

USB and Ethernet connection LEDs

If the LED indicates a problem with the relevant connection, check that the cable is securely connected at both ends.

Then go to the Device Manager and check that there are no problems with the modem. This will be listed in the Network Adapter category.

In the case of a USB connection, make sure that USB is enabled in the BIOS, as described on pages 158-159.

If you are using a cable modem, and it is connected via a signal splitter, so that you can connect the cable to another device such as a TV, remove the splitter and connect the modem directly to the cable input.

If the problem persists then try resetting the modem. Many computer problems can be fixed by the simple expedient of switching off for a few seconds and then restarting. This applies equally to broadband modems. Some modems will have a reset button on the front panel for this purpose.

However, power-cycling, i.e. switching off the PC, disconnecting the modem and then reconnecting it before switching the PC back on again, is a better approach to take. Doing it this way can address a range of hardware and software issues.

Hot tip

If you are using a cable network, consider the possibility that the network itself is down. You can easily establish this by checking your TV – if it's not receiving a signal, then neither is the modem.
    Alternatively, a phone call will quickly tell you what you need to know. Often, ISPs will play a recorded message detailing problem locations.

Hot tip

If there is no obvious cause of lack of connectivity, try power-cycling the modem. This will reset the device and very often does the trick.

Index

N

O

P

R

S

T